JEREMIAH
THE PROPHET BETWEEN CRACKS OF A BROKEN NATION

TEARS, FIRE, AND THE VOICE THAT WOULD NOT BE SILENCED

DAMIANO B. CENTOLA

EXPLORA BOOKS
700 – 838 West Hastings St. Vancouver
BC V6C 0A6
www.explorabooks.com
Phone: (604) 330 6795

No part of this book may be reproduced, stored in a retrieval system, or transmitted by any means without the written permission of the author.

Because of the dynamic nature of the Internet, any web addresses or links contained in this book may have changed since publication and may no longer be valid. The views expressed in this work are solely those of the author and do not necessarily reflect the views of the publisher, and the publisher hereby disclaims any responsibility for them.

Bible verses are quoted from the King James Version (KJV), which is public domain, the English Standard Version (ESV), and the New King James Version (NKJV).

ISBN: 978-1-83430-018-4 *(Paperback)*
978-1-83430-019-1 *(Hardback)*
978-1-83430-020-7 *(eBook)*

© 2025 Damiano B. Centola. All rights reserved

JEREMIAH

THE PROPHET BETWEEN
CRACKS OF A BROKEN NATION

TEARS, FIRE, AND THE VOICE THAT WOULD NOT BE SILENCED

DAMIANO B. CENTOLA

TABLE OF CONTENTS

DEDICATION..i
PREFACE..iii
INTRODUCTION v
   A Voice for the Hour Before the Fall ....
CHAPTER I 1
   The Call Before Collapse — A Prophet Is Formed..
CHAPTER II...7
   Burning Words in a Shaking World — Jeremiah's Fire Within ....
CHAPTER III...13
   False Prophets and Broken Altars — Exposing the Lie ....
CHAPTER IV...19
   The Temple Sermon — When Religion Becomes Rebellion......................
CHAPTER V...25
   The Yoke of Babylon — Submission as Sovereignty ....
CHAPTER VI...33
   The Scroll Was Burned — But the Word Returned.....................................
CHAPTER VII..39
   Weeping Over a City That Would Not Listen..
CHAPTER VIII..45
   The Potter's House — Vessels of Glory or Destruction ....
CHAPTER IX...51
   The Broken Covenant — Judah's Spiritual Adultery...................................
CHAPTER X...59
   Letters from Exile — Hope in Captivity ....
CHAPTER XI...67
   The Book of Consolation — A New Covenant Foretold ....
CHAPTER XII..75
   Jeremiah and the Remnant — The Ones Who Fled......................................

CHAPTER XIII 83
    Foreshadows of the Christ — The Righteous Branch ....

CHAPTER XIV 91
    The Prophet and the Pit — A Life of Rejection ....

CHAPTER XV 97
    Jeremiah's Final Word — The Cup of God's Wrath ....

APPENDIX 103

SCRIPTURE INDEX 105

GLOSSARY OF TERMS 109

ACKNOWLEDGEMENTS 113

ABOUT THE AUTHOR 115

DEDICATION

To the one who still weeps when truth is ignored.

To the voice who speaks even when no one listens.

To the soul standing in the cracks between collapse and hope.

This book is for the prophets who obey in obscurity,

for the scribes who write when scrolls are burned,

for the remnant who remain when all others flee.

And to the One who called me—

before I was formed,

before I was known,

before I had a voice.

To the Lord, who still speaks.

And to Feebe, who always listens.

— Damiano B. Centola

PREFACE

The Prophet No One Wanted, in a Time No One Understood

There are men who speak for God when the people are listening, and there are men who speak for God when no one wants to hear. Jeremiah was the latter. He was not welcomed into the courts of kings, nor was he lauded by religious councils. His scrolls were burned. His voice was mocked. His tears were seen as weakness, and his warnings were labeled treason. Yet he remained—rooted, obedient, unshakable.

Jeremiah lived in the thin place between warning and exile, between mercy and judgment, between the last trembling offer of covenant grace and the collapse of a nation's soul. He stood alone, but he was not abandoned. He was ridiculed, but not silenced. His name means "Yahweh will exalt," but his life was lived in the dust of collapse, in the ash of a burning city, and in the pain of divine rejection.

This book is not simply a study of Jeremiah—it is an entry into the furnace of a prophetic heart. It is a walk through the ruins of a society that once knew God but chose its own way. It is a mirror for our generation.

Jeremiah is the prophet between the cracks. Between Isaiah's lofty visions and Ezekiel's transcendent wheels, we find a man in chains, in tears, in fire, and in prayer. He weeps over Jerusalem. He wrestles with God. He pleads with kings. He writes what is burned and then writes it again. He delivers words that break the heart, and yet within his trembling voice is planted one of the most powerful seeds in Scripture—the promise of a New Covenant written not on tablets of stone, but on the human heart.

Our world today does not lack knowledge—it lacks conviction. It does not lack prophets—it lacks listeners. Jeremiah was called to speak when silence was popular and when truth was dangerous. This book is written for those who feel the stirrings of a similar call—for pastors, prophets, watchmen, and weeping intercessors in our own collapsing times.

Here you will meet not just a man, but a message. Not just a historical figure, but a timeless fire. Jeremiah did not volunteer for his assignment.

He was chosen before he was formed. He did not find comfort in his calling, but he found faithfulness in the God who called him.

The scrolls are still speaking.

The fire is still burning.

And in the cracks of our crumbling culture, the voice of Jeremiah rises again—not to entertain us, but to awaken us.

Let the reader not simply analyze this prophet. Let the reader listen.

Let the word burn again.

—Damiano B. Centola

INTRODUCTION
A Voice for the Hour Before the Fall

In every generation, God raises a voice that does not echo the times but confronts them. That voice often comes wrapped in rejection. It trembles with agony, not arrogance. It weeps before it warns. It prays even while it proclaims. Jeremiah was that voice.

He lived during a time of impending collapse—when the foundations of Jerusalem were cracking beneath the weight of idolatry, injustice, and indifference. The temple still stood, but its glory had fled. The priesthood functioned, but its conscience had died. The people proclaimed peace, but war was on the doorstep. And in the middle of it all stood a man God had formed before the womb, called before conception, and sent into a generation that would hate his every word.

Jeremiah's voice is not a distant relic—it is a divine reverberation that speaks with clarity into our own cultural hour. His world was one of confusion—where political compromise had infected spiritual leadership, and the prophetic was polluted by popularity and lies. Yet God did not leave His people without a warning. He raised up a man who would bleed, fast, cry, and confront—not with sword or spear, but with a scroll and a yoke.

Unlike Isaiah's poetic grandeur or Ezekiel's cosmic visions, Jeremiah's message was local, immediate, raw. He felt what God felt. He wept with the broken heart of heaven. His life embodied the groaning of divine grief. Yet even in judgment, he delivered glimmers of unmatched hope: of a returning remnant, a healing land, and a coming covenant where the law would no longer be written on stone but carved upon the human soul.

This book does not aim to retell history alone, but to awaken the reader to the living urgency of Jeremiah's call. The prophetic is not merely foretelling—it is forth-telling. It reveals the heart of God in the face of rebellion. It warns, but it also woos. Jeremiah's words were forged in prayer, in prison, in prophetic agony. And yet they endure because they carry the eternal breath of God.

We write at a time when nations tremble, when lies are louder than truth, when the temple is admired but the covenant is ignored. We live in an age of false peace, where the cry of "tolerance" has replaced the call to repentance, and where prophets are still silenced for saying what is unpopular but true.

Jeremiah was not merely a man with a message. He was the message. He lived the burden he carried. His tears were not theatrics. They were the visible grief of God expressed through a yielded vessel.

In these pages, we will walk through the life, laments, and legacy of a man who stood in the gap when the wall was breaking. We will listen to his words not as ancient warnings, but as living summons. We will uncover the burning core of a prophet who did not want the mantle—but carried it anyway.

Jeremiah is not finished speaking. His call is our call. His weeping is our intercession. His scroll has not been burned—it has been reopened for such a time as this.

May his cry awaken your ears.

May his yoke humble your pride.

May his hope restore your vision.

And may the fire that shut up in his bones ignite something in yours.

CHAPTER I
The Call Before Collapse — A Prophet Is Formed

"Before I formed thee in the belly I knew thee..."
— Jeremiah 1:5

There are moments in history when the voice of God cuts through the noise—not as a whisper, but as a divine interruption. For Jeremiah, that moment came not in a palace, not in a revival, but in the quiet obscurity of youth. He was not yet a man of influence, nor a prophet of renown. He was a priest's son in the small town of Anathoth. But the Word of the Lord came to him, and it would reshape the fate of nations.

Jeremiah was born during a transitional moment in Judah's history—a time when the winds of political reform blew through Jerusalem under King Josiah, but the spiritual decay ran deeper than public policy could reach. The idols may have been removed from the streets, but they were still enthroned in hearts. And it was into this smoldering contradiction that God called forth a prophet—one who would not only speak, but embody the grief and fire of the Most High.

Known Before Formed
"Before I formed thee in the belly I knew thee..."

These words are the cornerstone of Jeremiah's identity and the foundation of his ministry. God begins not with command, but with intimacy. The call of the prophet does not originate with Jeremiah's will, desire, or ability—it begins in the eternal counsel of God. Before flesh clothed his bones, before he opened his eyes, before his mother ever held him, Jeremiah was known.

The Hebrew word for "knew" (יָדַע – yada) denotes far more than awareness—it implies deep, covenantal relationship.

Jeremiah's life was not a product of chance or culture; it was a divine assignment woven into time by the hands of the Creator Himself. Before he was formed, he was chosen. Before he could speak, he was appointed.

This truth dismantles every modern argument that identity is self-made. In Jeremiah's call, we see the divine prerogative to consecrate, to set apart, to plant purpose before breath even fills the lungs. The prophet's voice did not rise out of ambition; it rose out of ordination.

The Weight of Divine Appointment

To be called by God is a sacred terror. Jeremiah does not respond with excitement, but with trembling. "Ah, Lord God! Behold, I cannot speak: for I am a child." His words echo the honest panic of the truly called. He does not rush to the spotlight. He recoils from it. His objection is not rebellion—it is reverence.

In the Hebrew, the word translated "child" (נַעַר – na'ar) can mean youth, servant, or even inexperienced one. Jeremiah's hesitation reveals a heart aware of the weight of divine speech. He knows that true prophets are not applauded—they are often despised. He knows that the words he will speak may cost him everything. And yet, God does not affirm Jeremiah's self-assessment.

God says, "Say not, I am a child… for thou shalt go to all that I shall send thee, and whatsoever I command thee thou shalt speak." The Lord silences Jeremiah's insecurity with sovereign authority. Heaven is not moved by earthly qualifications. God is not looking for ability, but availability. Jeremiah's call is not optional—it is inevitable.

Touched by Fire

"Then the Lord put forth his hand, and touched my mouth…"

This is the turning point. God does not merely command—He consecrates. He does not only send—He sanctifies. With a single gesture, the lips of Jeremiah are made holy ground. What was once a mouth of hesitation becomes a vessel of divine proclamation.

This image mirrors the experience of Isaiah, whose lips were touched with a coal from the altar (Isaiah 6:6–7). But unlike Isaiah, who responded with "Here am I, send me," Jeremiah had to be persuaded. His commissioning is not from a distance; it is personal. God places His own hand upon the prophet's mouth and declares, "Behold, I have put my words in thy mouth."

These are not suggestions. These are divine utterances—weighty, unalterable, dangerous. To speak them would be to carry judgment and mercy in one breath. Jeremiah would become the voice of both ruin and restoration.

The Prophet Set Over Nations

What follows is one of the most staggering declarations in all prophetic literature:

> *"See, I have this day set thee over the nations and over the kingdoms,*
>
> *to root out, and to pull down, and to destroy, and to throw down,*
>
> *to build, and to plant."*
>
> *— Jeremiah 1:10*

Jeremiah, a young man from a village outside Jerusalem, is suddenly placed over nations. Not with a throne, not with a sword, but with a word. His authority is not political—it is prophetic. He will not lead armies; he will confront them. He will not command by force; he will command by truth.

The sequence is deliberate: four actions of destruction—root out, pull down, destroy, throw down—followed by two actions of restoration—build and plant. Jeremiah's voice is forged first to confront, then to comfort. This pattern defines his ministry. He will speak into the fall of Jerusalem, the exile of Judah, the hypocrisy of the priests, and the deception of false prophets. But he will also speak of a returning remnant, a covenant written on hearts, and a Righteous Branch that shall rise.

Alone but Not Abandoned

Jeremiah's obedience will not earn him fame. It will cost him dearly.

> He will be rejected by his own townspeople in Anathoth (Jeremiah 11:21).

> He will be beaten and imprisoned by priests and officials (Jeremiah 20:2).

> He will be thrown into a cistern and left to die (Jeremiah 38:6).

> He will be dragged against his will to Egypt by a rebellious remnant (Jeremiah 43:1–7).

And yet, through it all, the voice of the Lord will not leave him. The fire will not go out. The burden will not lift. Jeremiah will be sustained not by applause, but by the unshakable presence of God.

> *"Be not afraid of their faces: for I am with thee to deliver thee, saith the Lord."*
>
> — *Jeremiah 1:8*

This promise becomes his anchor. When the scrolls are burned, the Lord tells him to write again. When no one listens, the Lord tells him to speak again. When his heart breaks, God shares in the grief. Jeremiah's ministry is not one of success by human standards—it is one of faithfulness under fire.

The Weeping Call

Jeremiah's life reveals something rare: a prophet who feels what God feels.

He is not a cold messenger. He is not a mechanical mouthpiece. He is a vessel of divine emotion. His tears are real. His grief is holy. His laments are Scripture. The same prophet who proclaims judgment also intercedes for mercy. The same mouth that rebukes kings also pleads for restoration. He carries both sword and balm, both fire and tears.

This duality is what makes Jeremiah prophetic in the highest sense—not simply because he foretells the future, but because he mirrors the heart of God. He is the living embodiment of divine sorrow over sin and divine hope for redemption.

Our Generation's Echo

In many ways, we stand in a similar hour. Institutions tremble. Morality is redefined. False peace is proclaimed from pulpits while truth is labeled divisive. The prophets of popularity still say, "All shall be well," while the warnings of Scripture groan beneath the surface.

Who will stand in the breach? Who will weep over the city before it burns?

Who will speak when silence is safe, and truth costs everything?

The call of Jeremiah is not bound to history—it is alive in every age. It is the call to be known before formed, to be touched before sent, to be faithful in the fire, and to speak when no one listens.

You may feel the stirring of that same fire shut up in your bones.

You may sense the trembling urgency to proclaim the Word, not for applause, but for obedience. If so, Jeremiah's story is not merely to be read—it is to be lived.

God is still calling prophets in the ruins.

He is still touching mouths.

He is still setting voices over nations.

And the collapse, though near, is never the end— For even in judgment, God plants the seeds of redemption.

CHAPTER II
Burning Words in a Shaking World — Jeremiah's Fire Within

> *"His word was in mine heart as a burning fire shut up in my bones..."*
> — *Jeremiah 20:9*

There is a difference between a man who speaks and a man who burns.

Jeremiah did not merely carry the Word of the Lord—he was consumed by it. His soul was not a scroll; it was a furnace. The words he received were not theoretical—they scorched him from the inside. He could not tame them, could not bury them, could not rest until he released them. But when he did, the cost was immediate. The prophet was despised, isolated, punished. The fire gave him no rest—but it also gave him no escape.

In a world that preferred smooth sayings and patriotic sermons, Jeremiah's words struck like lightning in a dry forest. Judah was already shaking—politically unstable, morally crumbling, and spiritually bankrupt. The kings were weak. The priests were corrupted. The prophets were bought. But Jeremiah? Jeremiah burned.

The Anatomy of the Fire

"Then I said, I will not make mention of Him, nor speak any more in His name…"

Jeremiah 20 records one of the most raw and vulnerable moments in prophetic literature. The prophet had been struck, bound, and publicly humiliated by Pashhur, the chief temple officer. The very place that should have honored the Word had become the instrument of its suppression. Jeremiah was not only bruised in body, but battered in soul. He had obeyed—and for his obedience, he was beaten.

In his anguish, Jeremiah makes a human decision: "I'm done." He resolves to be silent. He determines to suppress the burden. He chooses retreat. And for a moment, he tries. But what happens next is not the result of willpower or guilt—it is the eruption of divine fire:

> *"But His word was in mine heart as a burning fire shut up in my bones, and I was weary with forbearing, and I could not stay."*

This is not poetry. It is testimony. The fire of God's Word did not come from emotion or compulsion—it came from divine impartation. The Word itself had become a flame lodged inside his marrow. It did not ask permission to burn. It demanded release.

Jeremiah's fire was not born of charisma. It was born of communion. His isolation produced intimacy. His wounds produced revelation. He did not speak to be heard—he spoke because silence was suffocating.

Fire vs. Fear
The fire in Jeremiah's bones did not erase fear—but it outran it. He still trembled. He still wept. He still wished for death. But he burned anyway.

This is the difference between calling and ambition. Ambition seeks platforms. Calling endures prisons. Ambition performs. Calling bleeds. The fire in Jeremiah's bones was not self-made—it was God-given. And once touched by it, he could never be the same.

This burning is what separates true prophets from performers. False prophets invent words to gain attention. True prophets receive words that ruin their comfort. Jeremiah's fire was a crucible, not a spotlight. It purified him. It isolated him. It branded him.

The result? He could not stop.

"I heard the defaming of many, fear on every side…"

Yet the fire blazed on.

"All my familiars watched for my halting…"

Yet the fire surged deeper.

"Let us smite him with the tongue… let us not give heed to any of his words…"

Yet the fire rose louder.

The shaking world tried to suppress the prophet. But the fire within him would not be silenced.

A Fire That Doesn't Consume the Vessel

Unlike the fire of judgment that fell on Sodom, or the fire that devoured Nadab and Abihu, the fire in Jeremiah's bones was different. It did not destroy him. It refined him. It kept him alive. In a world of compromise, it preserved his conscience. In an age of dead religion, it made his voice thunder.

But it came at a cost.

Jeremiah was hated by the religious elite.

He was viewed as a traitor by nationalists.

He was a burden to kings and a byword to the people.

His name became synonymous with discomfort.

His message was unwelcome in every court. And yet, when he was thrown into the cistern, the fire burned even there. When he was left to starve, the fire still flamed.

God's Word was not just on his lips. It was in his bones.

This is the mystery of divine fire—it makes you weep and preach at once. It humbles you and strengthens you. It shatters your pride and steels your spine. You cannot boast in it, only bow beneath it.

The Danger of a Fireless Church

What happens when the Word is no longer fire? When sermons become strategies? When pulpits produce performances instead of prophets?

In Jeremiah's day, the priests said, "Peace, peace," when there was no peace. They declared safety when the sword was already at the gate. They traded fire for favor. And the people loved to have it so. But God had one man left burning. One man who refused to say what they wanted to hear.

Today, we face the same temptation. To dim the flame for fear of offense. To exchange the holy burden for public applause. But the Church does not need more echo chambers—it needs fire-bearers. It needs men and women who tremble under the Word, who cannot rest unless they declare it, who cry out in the streets even when the pews are empty.

Jeremiah was not trendy. He was terrifying. Not because he was cruel, but because he was holy. The fire in him was a mirror—and Judah could not bear to look.

Carriers of the Flame

You, reader, may feel this same holy disturbance. You have tried to be silent, but you cannot. You've attempted to fit in, but you no longer belong. You wake in the night with tears for a people who do not understand you. You weep in prayer for a Church that's forgotten its first love. You groan with a burden no one asked you to carry—but God placed it in your spirit.

You are not alone. Jeremiah was there first. And that fire? It is not there to torment you—it is there to send you.

You are not called to be impressive. You are called to be ignited.

This fire is not destructive—it is prophetic. It breaks chains. It exposes falsehood. It heals through holy confrontation. It speaks into shaking governments, trembling temples, and compromised hearts.

It is a fire that wakes the dead.

Fire in a Shaking World

Judah was shaking. Babylon was rising. Political alliances were failing. The temple was polluted. The priests were silent. The prophets were bought.

But God had a man with fire in his bones.

The same God still speaks. The same fire still falls. The Word is still burning—and it is looking for a vessel.

Let the fire return.

Let it burn in our pulpits.

Let it burn in our bones.

Let it burn in our prayers.

Let it burn in our tears.

Let it burn in the quiet, in the streets, in the pages of our journals.

Let it burn until we cannot stay silent. Let it burn until truth breaks through the fog.

This is not emotionalism. This is holiness.

The world is shaking. The altars are cracked.

And God is raising voices again—not polished, but burning.

CHAPTER III
False Prophets and Broken Altars — Exposing the Lie

Hananiah vs. Jeremiah — Truth Under Pressure
The collision was inevitable. Truth always meets resistance. And when the Word of the Lord burns in one man's bones, it will eventually confront the polished lies pouring from another man's lips.

Jeremiah stood in the temple courts with the burden of divine grief. His yoke of wood—a literal symbol he wore on his shoulders—declared submission to Babylon as God's judgment. It was not a message the people wanted. It was not patriotic. It was not positive. It was prophetic. And it placed him in direct opposition to the entire religious system.

Then came Hananiah.

Dressed in religious garb, speaking fluent temple language, standing beside Jeremiah as if an equal—Hananiah offered the people the message they longed to hear. It was fast. It was smooth. It was false.

The Two Voices in the Temple
Jeremiah 28 opens with a scene that looks, at first glance, like two prophets sharing opposing viewpoints. But it is more than a disagreement. It is a war between the Word of the Lord and the manipulations of man.

Hananiah speaks with confidence:

"Thus speaketh the Lord of hosts… I have broken the yoke of the king of Babylon."

He even sets a timeframe—"Within two full years…"—and follows with a dramatic act: breaking the wooden yoke off Jeremiah's shoulders in public view.

It's theater.

It's deceit.

It's what the people crave.

But heaven does not remain silent. Jeremiah, stunned yet composed, replies:

"Amen: the Lord do so…"

It sounds like agreement, but it's not. It's lament. He wishes it were true. He longs for peace. But he knows better. And so, after Hananiah finishes his performance, Jeremiah delivers the verdict:

"The prophet which prophesieth of peace, when the word of the prophet shall come to pass, then shall the prophet be known…"

And then:

"Hear now, Hananiah; The Lord hath not sent thee; but thou makest this people to trust in a lie."

The judgment is swift:

> *"This year thou shalt die, because thou hast taught rebellion against the Lord."*
>
> *And two months later, Hananiah was dead.*

When Comfort Becomes Treason

This confrontation is not merely historical—it is paradigmatic. It reveals the core crisis of every age: Who is speaking for God? Is it the one who brings comfort? Or the one who carries fire? Is it the smooth voice backed by crowds? Or the trembling one backed by Heaven?

False prophets always sound more appealing. They tell us what we want, not what we need. They cloak rebellion in blessing. They wrap judgment in denial. And their altars are crowded—because their gospel costs nothing.

But Jeremiah refuses to compromise. He does not retaliate with violence. He doesn't match Hananiah's theatrics. He simply stands, speaks, and obeys. Truth doesn't need embellishment. It needs endurance.

In Jeremiah's ministry, the false prophet is not a pagan. He is a fellow Israelite. He speaks in the temple. He uses the name of Yahweh. He mimics the style of the true. But his source is corrupted. His words are treason—not against the king, but against the God who ordained Babylon's rise.

This is the real danger: when falsehood wears the robes of religion, when rebellion dresses in prophecy, and when national pride replaces repentance.

Prophetic Theater vs. Prophetic Truth

The false prophet uses performance to manipulate perception. Hananiah broke the yoke Jeremiah had crafted as a living parable. The act was dramatic—but it was hollow. It mirrored the kind of prophetic style that gains popularity today: public spectacle, soundbites, bold predictions—but no intimacy with God, no secret place, no cost.

By contrast, Jeremiah's entire life was a prophecy. His pain was real. His yoke wasn't a gimmick—it was a divine instruction. He had to walk the streets with it. He carried the burden in silence until God released him to speak. His fire didn't seek a stage—it sought obedience.

There is a lesson here for every preacher, teacher, and voice in this generation:

Do not break the yoke unless God told you to.

Do not promise freedom when God is calling the nation to repentance.

Do not manufacture hope when judgment is knocking.

The altar of false prophecy is built on sand—and it always collapses.

Altars Built on Lies

Jeremiah's confrontation with Hananiah exposes more than just one man—it reveals the systemic infection of Judah's prophetic culture. It was not just Hananiah who was lying. It was an entire priesthood that had grown drunk on flattery. The altars were still burning incense, but the presence of God had departed. Sacrifices were being made, but without covenant fidelity. The temple became a stage, not a sanctuary.

Earlier in Jeremiah 5:31, the prophet records a piercing summary of the national condition:

> "The prophets prophesy falsely, and the priests bear rule by their means; and My people love to have it so: and what will ye do in the end thereof?"

It's not just the leaders—it's the people.

They wanted soft words. They wanted a quick rescue. They wanted a nationalistic god, not the God of righteousness.

So the prophets adapted. The priests adjusted. And the true Word of the Lord became offensive.

We see this today.

Altars that avoid repentance.

Sermons that baptize sin.

Movements that proclaim favor while ignoring disobedience.

But there is always a remnant.

And there is always a Jeremiah.

Prophets Who Refuse to Lie

To be a true prophet in a time of false prophecy is to walk a lonely road. Jeremiah's stand cost him honor, safety, friendship. But it secured for him the one thing that matters most: God's trust.

God could entrust Jeremiah with tears because Jeremiah didn't sell the truth.

He could entrust him with judgment because Jeremiah didn't soften the Word.

He could entrust him with restoration—because Jeremiah stayed faithful through the fire.

Today, the Church needs more Jeremiahs and fewer Hananiahs.

We need fewer forecasts of blessing without holiness.

Fewer declarations of destiny without submission.

Fewer promises of favor without repentance.

We need voices who will wear the yoke before they break it. Who will weep before they preach. Who will confront the lie not to shame, but to save.

Because the altar of lies is seductive. But it always leads to destruction.

The Word Will Prevail

Jeremiah's encounter with Hananiah ends with a grim sign: the false prophet dies. It is a terrifying reminder that God does not ignore misrepresentation. Speaking falsely in His name is not a branding opportunity—it's a death sentence.

But more than that, the moment proves this:

The Word of the Lord always prevails.

Hananiah's death may have been swift, but Jeremiah's message endured through the exile, through the captivity, through generations of silence, and into the New Covenant itself. The yoke may be broken, but the Word cannot be bound.

In the end, the voice that suffers is the voice that lasts.

The altar built on truth may be empty for a season—but it will stand when the others fall.

CHAPTER IV
The Temple Sermon — When Religion Becomes Rebellion

"Trust ye not in lying words, saying, The temple of the Lord, the temple of the Lord, the temple of the Lord, are these."

— Jeremiah 7:4

There are moments when God no longer addresses the streets—He speaks directly to the sanctuary.

The seventh chapter of Jeremiah is one of the most explosive moments in all prophetic literature. It is not delivered in the palace. It is not uttered in the market. It is not whispered in back alleys. It is proclaimed at the gate of the Temple of the Lord—the very center of Israel's national and religious identity.

God tells Jeremiah: "Stand in the gate of the Lord's house, and proclaim there this word…"

He is not to hide. He is not to soften. He is to shout the truth in the place where lies had taken root.

This is the Temple Sermon—a divine rebuke wrapped in covenant language, a fire-baptized confrontation against a people who believed their rituals could replace righteousness.

The Gate Where God Was Supposed to Dwell

Imagine the scene. Worshippers are arriving with sacrifices. Priests are walking in with incense. Levites are preparing the songs. The smell of burnt offering fills the air. There is structure, form, and reverence.

And in the middle of it all—Jeremiah, wild-eyed and fearless, calling out the words of the Lord:

"Amend your ways and your doings, and I will cause you to dwell in this place."

The people were convinced that as long as the temple stood, they were safe. They had conflated God's presence with the building, forgetting that the building without obedience becomes a shell. They recited phrases like charms—"The temple of the Lord, the temple of the Lord..."—as if saying the right words could silence their conscience.

But the temple had become a hiding place for sin. They assumed proximity to holiness meant approval from heaven.

God disagreed.

Religion Without Righteousness

Jeremiah tears through the veil of false security:

"Will ye steal, murder, and commit adultery, and swear falsely, and burn incense unto Baal... and come and stand before Me in this house... and say, We are delivered to do all these abominations?"

– Jeremiah 7:9–10

The prophet lists the very sins the people were committing—violence, sexual immorality, idolatry, covenant-breaking—and exposes the absurdity of their logic. They believed that their temple attendance granted them license to sin. That their sacrifices were sufficient to purchase divine approval. That worship excused rebellion.

This is not ancient history. This is the tragedy of every generation where religion is used to hide from God rather than to seek Him.

When liturgy becomes a mask for lawlessness, when rituals replace repentance, when temple culture substitutes for transformed character—rebellion is crowned with religious robes.

And the Lord will not dwell in such a house.

Shiloh: A Warning from the Past

To drive the point home, God reminds Judah of what happened at Shiloh—the first major sanctuary of Israel where the Ark of the Covenant once rested (see 1 Samuel 4). Shiloh had been destroyed because of Israel's sin.

> *"Go ye now unto My place which was in Shiloh… and see what I did to it for the wickedness of My people Israel."*
>
> — *Jeremiah 7:12*

This was a shocking comparison. Shiloh was gone—ruined, judged, desecrated. And now, God is saying: "Do not think this temple is immune. I will do to this house what I did to that one."

The implication was unbearable: Jerusalem itself was under the same judgment.

The sacred space would not save them. In fact, it would become a witness against them.

God does not play favorites. He honors covenant, not geography. He blesses obedience, not architecture.

When Intercession Is Shut

Perhaps the most chilling part of the Temple Sermon is not the warning—it's the command to Jeremiah:

> *"Therefore pray not thou for this people, neither lift up cry nor prayer for them, neither make intercession to Me: for I will not hear thee."*
>
> — *Jeremiah 7:16*

The intercessor is silenced.

The prophet, who weeps over his people, who pleads on their behalf, who carries the agony of divine mercy—is now told to stop.

Why? Because they had crossed a line. Their rebellion was no longer ignorance—it was willful. They were not confused—they were hardened. And in such moments, divine justice overtakes divine patience.

This is a sobering word. It reminds us that mercy is not endless in opportunity. God's longsuffering does not equal His approval. And when mercy is continually rejected, judgment is the only just response.

A Den of Robbers

Jesus would later echo this very sermon when He entered the temple in Jerusalem:

> *"It is written, My house shall be called the house of prayer; but ye have made it a den of thieves."*
>
> *— Matthew 21:13*

He was quoting Jeremiah 7.

Centuries after Jeremiah's cry, the same spirit had returned. Religious leaders were again exploiting the temple, merchandising the faith, and masking corruption with ceremony.

And again, the Lord arrived—not to celebrate their piety, but to turn over the tables.

This is the pattern:

- When the temple becomes performance, God sends prophets.
- When the sanctuary becomes a stage, God clears the room.
- When worship becomes empty, the fire leaves the altar.

Our Modern Temples

The message of Jeremiah 7 is not ancient—it is urgent.

Today, temples are not made of stone, but of platforms, ministries, and brands.

We sing, preach, and declare His name—yet injustice reigns, compromise thrives, and sin is excused under the banner of grace.

We chant our own versions of "the temple of the Lord…"

- "We are the church."
- "We have the truth."
- "We're under grace."
- "No condemnation here."

But the question still remains:

Have we amended our ways?

Have we turned from our idols?

Have we stopped the oppression of the fatherless, the widow, and the stranger?

Or have we simply decorated rebellion with Christian vocabulary?

A Call Back to True Worship

The temple is not a refuge for rebellion—it is the place of repentance.

God is not impressed by buildings or programs. He is looking for hearts that tremble at His Word.

In Isaiah 66:2, the Lord declares:

"To this man will I look, even to him that is poor and of a contrite spirit, and trembleth at My word."

That is the temple He desires. That is the worship He receives.

The Temple Sermon remains one of the most confrontational and necessary words for every generation:

- Tear down the altars of hypocrisy.
- Stop trusting in religious slogans.
- Return to the covenant.
- Clean the sanctuary.
- Let justice flow again.

Because if God was willing to leave Shiloh, and willing to tear down Solomon's temple—He is willing to walk away from any place that bears His name but not His holiness.

Let us examine our temples.

Let us test our doctrines.

Let us break before He must.

May our sanctuaries be sanctified.

May our altars burn again with righteousness, not ritual.

And may the gate of the Lord's house once again be filled with voices—not of marketing, but of repentance. Not of entertainment, but of fire.

CHAPTER V
The Yoke of Babylon
— Submission as Sovereignty

The hard message of surrender to survive
There are messages that uplift, and there are messages that undo.

Some prophecies come like rain after drought. Others come like thunder before a storm.

But none are as jarring—nor as theologically disruptive—as the word Jeremiah carried regarding Babylon.

Submit.

Surrender.

Go into exile.

Do not resist the judgment of God.

This was the prophet's message to the nation of Judah in its final years.

It sounded like treason.

It felt like heresy.

But it was the Word of the Lord.

In one of the most misunderstood and radical revelations in the history of Israel, God used Jeremiah to declare that the path to preservation would come through submission—not resistance. Babylon was not merely an enemy empire—it was a tool in the hands of divine justice.

The Wooden Yoke
In Jeremiah 27, the prophet is instructed by God to create a physical symbol:

> *"Make thee bonds and yokes, and put them upon thy neck..."*
>
> — *Jeremiah 27:2*

Imagine it—a prophet walking through the streets of Jerusalem, wearing a yoke like an ox. It was more than symbolic. It was scandalous. Yokes were worn by beasts, slaves, and captives. And now, the man who speaks for God is wearing one.

This yoke did not declare freedom—it declared bondage.

Not victory—judgment.

Not deliverance—discipline.

Jeremiah stood in the temple, yoke on his shoulders, and proclaimed not only to Judah but to the surrounding nations:

> *"Submit yourselves to the king of Babylon... bring your necks under the yoke... and live."*
>
> — *Jeremiah 27:12*

The message was clear: You will not escape Babylon. You must go through it.

This was not because God had changed His character. It was because His people had hardened their hearts. The covenant had been violated, the prophets had lied, the priests had compromised, and now the only way forward was through divine correction.

The Sovereignty of a Strange Plan
For many, the idea that God would use a pagan empire to accomplish His will seemed impossible. How could the God of Israel hand over His holy city to idolaters?

But this is the scandal of sovereignty: God will use whatever means necessary to fulfill His purposes.

Babylon's rise was not an accident. It was ordained.

> *"And now have I given all these lands into the hand of Nebuchadnezzar the king of Babylon, My servant..."*
>
> —*Jeremiah 27:6*

God calls Nebuchadnezzar "My servant."

Not because he was righteous. Not because he knew the Lord. But because he was being used by the Lord.

This shakes our theology. We want a God who only uses clean instruments. But the God of Scripture uses ravens to feed prophets, serpents to humble kings, foreign armies to discipline nations, and crosses to redeem the world.

Sovereignty does not consult our comfort. It fulfills God's will.

Resistance Is Futile

Jeremiah's message clashed with the nationalist prophets of his day. While others were prophesying victory, restoration, and the short-term defeat of Babylon, Jeremiah was declaring long captivity.

> *"Serve the king of Babylon, and live: wherefore should this city be laid waste?"*
>
> *— Jeremiah 27:17*

To resist would mean annihilation.

To fight back would be to fight against God Himself.

To surrender would mean survival—not escape from judgment, but endurance through it.

This was not cowardice—it was prophetic obedience.

God was not offering deliverance from captivity. He was offering deliverance through it.

This message was deeply offensive to the people, especially the leaders. Their pride, their theology, and their identity were tied to the idea of being God's chosen people. Surely God would never allow Jerusalem to fall. Surely He would not let the temple be burned.

But their hearts had already fallen. The covenant had already been forsaken. And the fire that would consume the temple was a reflection of the fire they had extinguished from their own altars.

The Yoke Broken by Hananiah
Enter Hananiah.

In Jeremiah 28, the false prophet publicly opposes Jeremiah's message by breaking the wooden yoke off his neck. It was dramatic. It was public. It was deceitful.

> *"Thus saith the Lord; Even so will I break the yoke of Nebuchadnezzar..."*
> — *Jeremiah 28:11*

But the Lord was not speaking through Hananiah.

He was lying.

And so, God responds by telling Jeremiah to make a yoke of iron—unbreakable, inescapable.

And Hananiah would die that same year for his rebellion.

This moment seals the truth: No amount of religious optimism can override divine sovereignty.

When God declares a season of correction, no prophecy, no program, and no politician can undo it.

A Theology of Exile
Jeremiah's message about Babylon was not just political—it was theological.

The people of Judah believed that the presence of the temple guaranteed God's favor. But Jeremiah revealed the deeper truth: God is not bound to buildings. He is bound to His covenant.

And when the covenant is broken, God's justice must be fulfilled—even if it means sending His people into exile.

But exile is not the end.

In the midst of these hard words, Jeremiah also declares:

> *"I know the thoughts that I think toward you, saith the Lord, thoughts of peace, and not of evil, to give you an expected end."*
> — *Jeremiah 29:11*

This famous verse is not a general encouragement. It is a promise to exiles. It is spoken to people who are about to lose everything—but not lose God.

Exile was not abandonment. It was refinement. It was the pruning of pride. The crushing of idolatry. The purification of a remnant. It was a severe mercy.

And that mercy still burns through Jeremiah's message today.

When Surrender Is Strength

In the Kingdom of God, strength is not always resistance—it is discernment.

To know when to fight and when to yield.

To know when to cry out for deliverance and when to bow under discipline.

Jeremiah did not call the people to give up.

He called them to give in—to submit to the hand of God, even when it came dressed in the armor of Babylon.

This is the test of true faith:

Can you trust God when He disciplines you?

Can you submit to correction when it comes through strange vessels?

Can you wear the yoke and still believe He has a plan to restore you?

Jeremiah did.

And he wore that yoke, not as a prisoner—but as a prophet.

He bore the shame of obedience while others basked in the applause of deception.

But in the end, it was Jeremiah who survived.

It was Jeremiah who heard from God in the ruins.

It was Jeremiah who lived to write the scroll of consolation and promise.

The Yoke Today

We still wear yokes—of culture, of consequence, of God's refining fire.

But not all yokes are curses.

Jesus said,

> *"Take My yoke upon you... for My yoke is easy, and My burden is light."*
> *— Matthew 11:29-30*

This is the irony: the only true freedom comes through surrender.

The only path to peace is under His lordship.

Even if He leads us through Babylon.

So wear the yoke.

Embrace the discipline.

Trust the sovereignty of a God who corrects in love, and who restores after the storm.

Because submission to Him is never defeat—it is the doorway to redemption.

CHAPTER VI
The Scroll Was Burned — But the Word Returned

Baruch, the scribe, and the unquenchable voice of God
You can burn the scroll, but you cannot silence the Word.

That is the central truth of Jeremiah chapter 36—a moment of profound confrontation between earthly power and eternal truth. In this chapter, we find a king with a knife, a scroll with fire, a scribe with trembling hands, and a prophet with tears in his eyes. It is a drama that unfolds not in the streets, but in the palace—a place where decisions are made in secret chambers and edicts are signed with seals.

But one thing becomes clear by the end: heaven writes faster than man can burn.

The Scroll Is Written
The story begins with an instruction from God:

> "Take thee a roll of a book, and write therein all the words that I have spoken unto thee against Israel, and against Judah... from the days of Josiah even unto this day."
>
> — *Jeremiah 36:2*

This was not a casual project. This was a sacred transcript—a written record of decades of divine speech. A prophetic autobiography of judgment, mercy, lament, and hope. And it had to be delivered not just through the prophet's mouth, but through the prophet's pen.

Jeremiah, likely under restriction or threat, dictates the entire message to his scribe, Baruch the son of Neriah. Day after day, word after word, fire after fire—the scroll is born. And it is carried with trembling hands to the temple and eventually to the ears of the king.

Baruch, though lesser known than Jeremiah, plays a vital role in prophetic history. He is the silent partner of divine revelation—the one who writes what others fear to hear. His name means "blessed," and yet his life is one of sorrow and risk.

A King with a Knife

When the scroll is finally read before King Jehoiakim, the drama intensifies. It is winter. The fire is burning in the hearth. The court officials are seated. The Word of the Lord echoes through the chamber.

And what does the king do?

> *"It came to pass, that when Jehudi had read three or four leaves, he cut it with the penknife, and cast it into the fire..."*
>
> *— Jeremiah 36:23*

Slice. Burn. Repeat.

Each portion of the scroll is destroyed as it is read.

This is not mere rejection. This is defiance.

Jehoiakim does not tear his garments in repentance—he tears God's Word in contempt.

He does not tremble—he scorches.

He does not question his ways—he destroys the very record of God's warnings.

This is more than a political act. It is theological warfare.

Jehoiakim represents every ruler who believes their throne is higher than God's.

Every heart that thinks truth can be edited.

Every soul that thinks Scripture can be censored.

But what burns in a fireplace cannot erase what burns in eternity.

The Word Returns

As soon as the scroll is destroyed, God speaks again:

> *"Take thee again another roll, and write in it all the former words that were in the first roll, which Jehoiakim the king of Judah hath burned..."*
>
> *— Jeremiah 36:28*

God does not panic. He does not revise. He commands a rewriting.

This time, He even adds more:

> *"And there were added besides unto them many like words."*
>
> — *Jeremiah 36:32*

This is the divine response to rebellion: the Word returns, stronger than before.

You can burn the scroll, but you cannot burn the truth.

You can silence the prophet, but you cannot stop the prophecy.

You can reject the warning, but you cannot avoid the consequence.

Jehoiakim thought he had the final word.

But the final word always belongs to the Lord.

The Preservation of the Word

What happened in that fire-heated room has echoed through history:

- Pharaoh rejected Moses' words—but God split the sea.
- Ahab imprisoned Micaiah—but the dogs still licked his blood.
- Herod silenced John the Baptist—but the kingdom advanced.
- Rome crucified Christ—but the tomb was rolled open.

The Word of the Lord is not fragile. It is not dependent on ink and parchment. It is living and eternal.

> *"The grass withereth, the flower fadeth: but the word of our God shall stand for ever."*
>
> — *Isaiah 40:8*

> *"Heaven and earth shall pass away, but My words shall not pass away."*
>
> — *Matthew 24:35*

Even today, as modern kings and digital emperors attempt to suppress, alter, or erase God's truth, the scroll is rewritten. The Spirit speaks. The message lives on.

The question is not whether the Word will survive.

The question is whether we will listen.

Baruch's Hidden Faithfulness

Behind the scenes of this chapter is a man whose hands trembled—but whose obedience endured.

Baruch, Jeremiah's scribe, stands as a model of hidden faithfulness.

- He wrote the Word that was burned.
- He wrote it again when God commanded.
- He fled with Jeremiah when the danger grew.
- He bore the cost of association with a hated prophet.

In Jeremiah 45, Baruch himself receives a word from God. He had grown weary. He had cried out in discouragement:

"Woe is me now! for the Lord hath added grief to my sorrow…"

But God reassures him:

> *"Seekest thou great things for thyself? seek them not… but thy life will I give unto thee for a prey."*

Baruch is promised survival—not fame.

Life—not prominence.

Obscurity—not greatness.

But in heaven's eyes, his ink preserved fire. His hands carried judgment and hope. His obedience kept the record alive.

Every generation needs its Baruchs—faithful scribes who carry the truth behind the curtain, who write what God says even when no one is listening, who preserve the Word when kings are burning it.

When the Scroll Is in You

In Jeremiah's time, the Word had to be written again.

But God had already promised a day when it would not be written on scrolls alone—but on hearts.

> *"I will put My law in their inward parts, and write it in their hearts…"*
> *— Jeremiah 31:33*

This is the ultimate fulfillment of what Jehoiakim tried to destroy: a Word that cannot be burned because it burns from within.

Jesus Christ, the living Word, is not written on parchment. He is written on the lives of His people.

And the Spirit of God now inscribes the truth not in ink, but in flame upon the soul.

This is what makes the Church unstoppable.

This is why every persecutor fails.

This is how the Gospel endures through war, censorship, imprisonment, and time.

The Word lives.

And it returns.

And it speaks still.

So let the kings burn their scrolls.

Let the proud draw their knives.

Let the age mock the prophets and dismiss the scribes.

But remember:

The Word will come again.

It will be written again.

It will never return void.

CHAPTER VII
Weeping Over a City That Would Not Listen

Jeremiah's lament vs. Jerusalem's stubbornness
There is no voice in Scripture that cries quite like Jeremiah.

Prophets are often associated with fire, fury, and judgment. They confront kings, tear down idols, and thunder divine decrees. But Jeremiah adds a sound not always heard in the prophetic chorus—the sound of weeping. His tears are not rhetorical. They are not for effect. They are real, raw, relentless. They stream from a heart that carries the grief of God Himself.

Jeremiah did not only speak for the Lord. He felt with the Lord.

He was the prophet who wept.

Not because he was weak. But because his heart had been shattered by the weight of a message that the people refused to hear.

A City Deaf to Heaven
The tragedy of Jeremiah's ministry was not simply that judgment was coming. It was that the people could have avoided it—if only they had listened.

Repeatedly, the prophet pleads:

"Hear ye the word of the Lord…"

"Amend your ways…"

"Return unto Me…"

"Obey My voice…"

But the ears of Jerusalem were closed.

> *"From the thirteenth year of Josiah... even unto this day... rising early and speaking; but ye have not hearkened."*
>
> — *Jeremiah 25:3*

They did not listen in the courts.

They did not listen in the streets.

They did not listen in the temple.

They did not listen to the scrolls, to the sermons, or to the signs.

The people of Judah were not merely rebellious—they were tone-deaf to truth. They had grown skilled in selective hearing, receiving what pleased them, and ignoring what convicted them.

They wanted prophets who affirmed, not ones who wept.

They wanted messages that soothed, not ones that warned.

They wanted peace when judgment was pounding on the gates.

And so, Jeremiah cried.

The Tears of a Prophet

> *"Oh that my head were waters, and mine eyes a fountain of tears, that I might weep day and night..."*
>
> — *Jeremiah 9:1*

This was not metaphor. It was soul-deep pain.

Jeremiah's grief was so profound that he begged for more tears—as if his own body could no longer contain the sorrow he carried. He wept not for personal loss, but for a people bent on destruction.

He grieved the daughters of Zion.

He mourned the fall of Jerusalem before it happened.

He cried for the slain of his people—not only for their future deaths, but for their present deafness.

In chapter 8, the prophet laments:

> *"Is there no balm in Gilead? Is there no physician there? Why then is not the health of the daughter of my people recovered?"*
>
> — *Jeremiah 8:22*

It is the cry of a heartbroken intercessor. He sees the disease. He knows the cure. But the patient refuses treatment.

The tears of Jeremiah echo the tears of Jesus centuries later:

> *"O Jerusalem, Jerusalem... how often would I have gathered thy children together... and ye would not!"*
>
> *— Matthew 23:37*

Same city.

Same stubbornness.

Same sorrow.

The Theology of Tears

Why did Jeremiah weep?

Because God weeps.

The tears of Jeremiah are not weakness—they are mirrors. They reflect the heart of a God who is just and yet grieved. God does not judge with delight. He warns. He pleads. He waits. But when the people harden their hearts, the sorrow of the Lord becomes visible in the voice of His prophet.

Jeremiah shows us that true prophetic ministry is never detached. It is not cold correction. It is not professional critique. It is compassionate confrontation.

The prophet is not just a mouth. He is a heart.

And that heart must be broken before it can carry the Word.

The Cost of Carrying Grief

Jeremiah's tears were not private. They were public. And they became a source of ridicule.

> *"I am in derision daily, every one mocketh me."*
>
> *— Jeremiah 20:7*

The people saw his emotion as instability. His passion as foolishness. His grief as weakness.

But grief is not weakness.

It is what happens when truth collides with love.

It is what happens when a prophet sees not just the sin—but the person behind the sin.

It is what happens when heaven shares its sorrow with earth.

Jeremiah did not enjoy his calling.

He did not celebrate the judgment.

He did not relish being right.

He wept.

Because love mourns when truth is rejected.

A Model for Modern Prophets

We live in an age saturated with voices. Social platforms are crowded with opinions, rebukes, and religious commentary. But how many of those voices weep?

- Who mourns over the sin they confront?
- Who trembles before the Word they proclaim?
- Who fasts and intercedes in secret before they speak in public?

Jeremiah reminds us that true authority flows not from volume, but from brokenness.

The prophet who has not wept should not speak.

The minister who has not mourned should not preach judgment.

The teacher who lacks tears may speak truth—but he will miss the heart of God.

We must raise up voices that weep before they warn.

Because that is what our generation needs—not louder preachers, but deeper ones.

Not harsher critics, but holier intercessors.

God Still Weeps

The tears of Jeremiah echo through the book of Lamentations, where the prophet composes five chapters of poetic mourning over the fall of Jerusalem.

He does not say "I told you so."

He does not retreat into bitterness.

He lays on the ruins and weeps.

He intercedes from the ashes.

He becomes the voice of God's broken heart.

And yet, even in his lament, a new word rises:

> *"It is of the Lord's mercies that we are not consumed, because His compassions fail not. They are new every morning..."*
>
> — *Lamentations 3:22-23*

Hope.

Still there.

Even in the rubble.

Because the God who weeps is also the God who restores.

And the prophet who mourns becomes the messenger of mercy.

CHAPTER VIII
The Potter's House
— Vessels of Glory or Destruction

Can the clay say to the potter?
There are moments in a prophet's life when God doesn't merely speak to him—He shows him.

One day, the word of the Lord comes to Jeremiah in a different form—not a sermon, not a scroll, not a thunderous declaration. This time, it is an image—simple, earthy, and unforgettable.

> *"Arise, and go down to the potter's house, and there I will cause thee to hear My words."*
>
> *—Jeremiah 18:2*

The instruction is deliberate. God does not say, "Listen here." He says, "Go and see." Jeremiah is sent on a field trip of revelation—to the workshop of a humble craftsman shaping vessels of clay.

And what he sees becomes a divine parable of judgment, mercy, sovereignty, and the fragile will of man.

The Potter and the Wheel
Jeremiah walks in quietly and watches.

The potter is at work. The wheel is spinning. The clay is soft. His hands are wet. The process is ancient, rhythmic, almost sacred.

And then something happens.

The vessel he is shaping becomes marred in his hand.

It collapses. It twists. It refuses form.

But the potter doesn't throw it away.

He reshapes it—makes it again into another vessel, as it seems good to him.

At this moment, God speaks:

> "O house of Israel, cannot I do with you as this potter? saith the Lord."
>
> "Behold, as the clay is in the potter's hand, so are ye in Mine hand…"
>
> —Jeremiah 18:6

It is a breathtaking declaration.

It affirms both divine sovereignty and human fragility.

It confirms that God shapes nations as potters shape clay.

But it also raises a haunting question:

What happens when the clay resists the hand of the Potter?Marred in the Potter's Hand

The image of the marred vessel is key.

The Hebrew word used for "marred" (נִשְׁחַת – nishchat) implies ruin, corruption, or damage beyond use. It's not simply a misshapen pot—it's a symbol of a people who have hardened, resisted, and disobeyed.

God does not discard the clay immediately.

He reworks it.

He starts again.

He seeks to shape it into something else.

This reveals His mercy. His patience. His desire to redeem what was spoiled.

But this mercy is not infinite in opportunity.

In the next verses, the Lord warns:

> "At what instant I shall speak concerning a nation… to pluck up, and to pull down, and to destroy it…"
>
> "If that nation… turn from their evil, I will repent of the evil…"
>
> "And at what instant I shall speak… to build and to plant it…"
>
> "If it do evil… then I will repent of the good…"

This is divine contingency.

God is sovereign, but He allows space for human response.

He holds the clay, but the clay has a will. Vessels of Destruction or Glory

Paul echoes this metaphor centuries later in Romans 9, referring to humanity as vessels made for either wrath or mercy. But here in Jeremiah, the emphasis is not predestination—it is moral responsibility.

The vessel is not chosen for destruction arbitrarily.

It becomes so by resistance.

Jerusalem had been a vessel of beauty. Chosen. Fashioned. Anointed. But now it was resisting the shaping hand of God. Instead of yielding, it rebelled. Instead of trusting, it stiffened.

God's message through Jeremiah is clear:

> *"I am still shaping you. But if you will not yield—then judgment is what I must shape."*

This is one of the most terrifying truths of Scripture:

You will be shaped.

Either as a vessel of glory—or a vessel of judgment.

Either by surrender—or by fire.

The Potter's Right

God does not apologize for His sovereignty.

> *"Behold, as the clay is in the potter's hand, so are ye in Mine hand..."*
>
> — *Jeremiah 18:6*

This is the holy tension:

- God is sovereign.
- We are responsible.
- He can reshape—but He will not override forever.
- He is patient—but not passive.
- He is merciful—but not manipulable.

And when a people resist, resist, resist… there comes a point when the shaping ends—and the smashing begins.

In Jeremiah 19, the next chapter, the prophet is told to take a fired clay vessel and break it in front of the people:

> *"Even so will I break this people and this city..."*
>
> *— Jeremiah 19:11*

Why?

Because fired clay cannot be reshaped.

It is too late. It must be broken.

This is the progression:

1. Soft clay — God can shape.
2. Resistant clay — God tries to reshape.
3. Hardened vessel — God must break.

The Potter Is Still Shaping

Today, the wheel still turns.

God still shapes nations.

He still speaks through prophets.

> He still sends warnings, offers mercy, reaches out with wet hands and patient voice.

But the clay must yield.

- The Church must yield.
- The heart must soften.
- The nation must bow.
- The soul must surrender.

The wheel is spinning faster than ever.

The world is being shaped by powers and principalities, but God is still the true Potter.

And He is not finished.

But the question remains:

Will we let Him shape us? Or will we harden against His touch?

Surrender to the Shaping

The potter is not cruel.

He does not crush without reason.

He does not discard without cause.

But He is holy.

And He will not shape a vessel that refuses to be made.

Let us return to the wheel.

Let us yield to the hands.

Let us surrender before we harden.

Let us cry out before we crack.

Because the Potter is not finished.

He still has vessels to form—Vessels of righteousness.

Vessels of glory.

Vessels fit for the Master's use.

CHAPTER IX
The Broken Covenant
— Judah's Spiritual Adultery

"They have turned their back unto Me, and not their face..."
— Jeremiah 2:27

When a marriage is betrayed, it is not only a violation of commitment—it is the severing of intimacy. The book of Jeremiah is not merely a record of national rebellion; it is a divine lament over covenant infidelity. Judah had not just sinned—she had cheated. She had played the harlot under every green tree. She had sought pleasure in foreign gods. And the Lord—her covenant Husband—was heartbroken.

From the opening chapters of Jeremiah, we are drawn into a love story gone tragically wrong. The language is piercing, poetic, and painfully personal.

"I remember thee, the kindness of thy youth, the love of thine espousals, when thou wentest after Me in the wilderness..."
— Jeremiah 2:2

It begins with remembrance. God recalls the early days—when Israel followed Him through the desert, clung to Him in the unknown, and vowed loyalty. But now, she has grown cold. Enticed. Unfaithful.

What began as a covenant has devolved into adultery.

Turning Backs, Not Faces
Perhaps no image is more indicting than this:

"They have turned their back unto Me, and not their face..."
— Jeremiah 2:27

This is not just neglect—it is intentional rejection.

To turn one's back to God is to say:

> *"I no longer want to see You. I no longer want to hear You. I will direct my life as I please."*

It is the breaking of a gaze.

The severing of communion.

The refusal of relationship.

Judah had not simply failed to live up to God's expectations—she had walked away from Him.

And yet, in moments of crisis, she still cried out:

> *"Arise, and save us!"*
>
> — *Jeremiah 2:27*

The hypocrisy is staggering.

They abandoned the covenant—but demanded protection.

They rejected the Word—but expected blessing.

This is the madness of spiritual adultery: to forsake the marriage and still expect the benefits of it.

Broken Cisterns

One of the most powerful metaphors in Jeremiah 2 is this:

> *"For My people have committed two evils; they have forsaken Me the fountain of living waters, and hewed them out cisterns, broken cisterns, that can hold no water."*
>
> — *Jeremiah 2:13*

It is not just that Judah walked away from God—they tried to replace Him.

They traded living water for leaking wells.

They exchanged the divine for the dead.

They attempted to fill their souls with the gods of wood and stone.

But idols cannot speak.

They cannot save.

They cannot love.

They are broken vessels—just like the hearts that chase them.

And yet the people persisted.

> *"As the thief is ashamed when he is found, so is the house of Israel ashamed... saying to a stock, Thou art my father; and to a stone, Thou hast brought me forth."*
>
> *— Jeremiah 2:26-27*

They were bowing to lifeless things.

Worshiping what they had made with their own hands.

And calling it "god."

The covenant was not just broken—it was mocked.

A Nation Shameless

Jeremiah cries out:

> *"Were they ashamed when they had committed abomination? Nay, they were not at all ashamed, neither could they blush..."*
>
> *— Jeremiah 6:15*

This is one of the most terrifying signs of covenant decay: the loss of shame.

When sin no longer stings,

When conscience no longer convicts,

When what is holy is mocked and what is profane is praised—

the soul is already in judgment.

Judah had not only forsaken God—she forgot how to blush.

And the Lord, her faithful Husband, was no longer welcome in His own house.

> *"My house is full of deceit..."*
>
> *"They lie in wait, as he that setteth snares..."*
>
> *"Shall I not visit for these things?"*
>
> *— Jeremiah 5:26-29*

The tone shifts. The weeping begins to burn. Divine sorrow prepares for divine judgment.

But even then—God pleads.

The Unrelenting Mercy of a Husband

> *"Turn, O backsliding children, saith the Lord; for I am married unto you..."*
>
> — *Jeremiah 3:14*

This is the astonishing grace of the covenant:

Even when betrayed, God still claims His people.

Even when abandoned, He offers restoration.

"I am married to you."

He does not file for divine divorce.

He extends His hand again.

Return.

Confess.

Come back.

> *"Only acknowledge thine iniquity, that thou hast transgressed against the Lord thy God..."*
>
> — *Jeremiah 3:13*

God was not seeking performance—He was seeking repentance.

He was not demanding penance—He was asking for honesty.

He was willing to restore—but only if they returned.

The covenant may have been broken—but it was not beyond repair.

The Prophetic Parallel: Hosea and the Unfaithful Bride

Jeremiah's language parallels that of Hosea, the prophet who was commanded to marry a prostitute as a living symbol of Israel's spiritual adultery.

Gomer, the unfaithful wife, chased other lovers.

Hosea, the faithful husband, redeemed her again and again.

This was not only Hosea's burden.

It was God's heart.

> *"How shall I give thee up, Ephraim? How shall I deliver thee, Israel?... My heart is turned within Me..."*
>
> — *Hosea 11:8*

Jeremiah weeps with the same fire.

His warnings are not cold—they are the cries of a wounded Bridegroom.

God does not want Judah destroyed.

He wants her restored.

But restoration requires repentance.

And repentance requires recognition of betrayal.

Until the covenant is acknowledged as broken, it cannot be healed.

Our Covenant Crisis

We too live in an age of covenant confusion.

- Churches bear His name but deny His lordship.
- Nations claim His blessings but reject His commands.
- Individuals cry for grace but despise holiness.

We want the benefits of the covenant without the boundaries.

We want the blessings of the marriage while living like adulterers.

And yet God still calls:

"Return unto Me…"

"I am married to you…"

"Only acknowledge your iniquity…"

He is not the God of performance—He is the God of return.

Not the God of shame—but the God of holy love.

But the time for return is not indefinite.

When covenant love is refused too long, judgment must come.

Turn Your Face Again

The final image remains:

> *"They have turned their back unto Me, and not their face."*

Let that not be said of us.

Let us turn our face again to the One who formed us.

Let us remember the love of our youth.

Let us forsake the idols.

Let us come back to the covenant.

Let us be faithful again.

Because the Bridegroom still waits.

The marriage is not over.

But the window is closing.

Let us turn—not our backs, but our hearts.

Let us return—not in word only, but in soul.

Let us remember—He is still married to us.

אנכי ידעתי את המחשבות אשר אנכי חשב ליכם

בוריך הדשר

CHAPTER X
Letters from Exile — Hope in Captivity

"For I know the thoughts that I think toward you..."
— *Jeremiah 29:11*

The city was burning. The temple was in ruins. The royal line was broken. And the people of Judah were now captives in Babylon—a foreign land of strange gods, unfamiliar customs, and remembered shame.

From the moment Jeremiah began to prophesy, exile was the message no one wanted to hear. And now it had come.

But the astonishing truth is this: when the people were at their lowest, God sent a letter.

Not a sword.

Not a plague.

Not another punishment.

A letter.

A message from heaven through the hand of the prophet—sent across borders and beneath oppression. It did not arrive with trumpet or thunder, but with ink, parchment, and divine mercy.

In Jeremiah 29, we find the letter to the exiles. And within it, some of the most famous and most misquoted words in all of Scripture.

But before we quote them, we must understand them.

Reality in Babylon

The false prophets were still speaking—even in exile.

Some were claiming the captivity would be short. Others promised a swift return. Religious optimism thrived even in foreign soil.

But God was not offering a shortcut. He was offering stability in the storm.

> "Build ye houses, and dwell in them; and plant gardens, and eat the fruit of them..."
>
> "Take ye wives... be increased there, and not diminished..."
>
> "Seek the peace of the city whither I have caused you to be carried away captives..."
>
> — Jeremiah 29:5-7

This was a hard word.

God was telling them: Settle down. This exile is not ending tomorrow.

It was not the word they wanted. But it was the word they needed. Because sometimes the fastest way back is to stop trying to escape.

Instead of resisting reality, they were to embrace it—with hope.

They were to build, not despair.

Plant, not scatter.

Pray for the city, not curse it.

Raise families, not shrink in fear.

Invest in the land, not waste away in mourning.

Babylon was not their final destination. But it was their current assignment.

And peace would come—not through escape, but through obedience.

The False Promise of Easy Deliverance

In the same breath, God rebukes the liars:

> "Let not your prophets and your diviners... deceive you... they prophesy falsely unto you in My name: I have not sent them."
>
> — Jeremiah 29:8-9

The false prophets had told the people what they wanted to hear:
- "This won't last long."
- "God will deliver you any day now."
- "You'll be back home before you know it."

But that wasn't hope. That was deception.

Hope based on a lie is no hope at all. It's a setup for disillusionment.

Jeremiah's letter did not deny the pain—but it rooted their perspective in the plan of God.

Seventy Years

> *"For thus saith the Lord, That after seventy years be accomplished at Babylon I will visit you, and perform My good word toward you..."*
>
> *— Jeremiah 29:10*

Seventy years.

Two generations.

Enough time for those who entered exile to die there.

Enough time for children to grow up never knowing Jerusalem.

Enough time for the land to rest from idolatry and bloodshed.

This was not punishment alone—it was reset. A Sabbath for the land and a purification of the people. Seventy years to remember the covenant they had forsaken.

But it would not last forever.

God would visit them again. And He would bring them home.

The Promise in Exile

Now we arrive at the verse known by so many—and misunderstood by even more:

> *"For I know the thoughts that I think toward you, saith the Lord, thoughts of peace, and not of evil, to give you an expected end."*
>
> *— Jeremiah 29:11*

This was not spoken to the comfortable.

This was not addressed to the free.

This was a letter to slaves—to exiles, to families who had lost everything.

And yet God says: I know My thoughts toward you.

When they didn't know how to think about their future, God already had it planned.

- Thoughts of peace — even in a war-torn land.
- Not of evil — even though judgment had fallen.
- An expected end — even when the present was unbearable.

This is the unshakable promise of covenant mercy:

God's thoughts are not scattered. They are sovereign.

He has not forgotten. He has not abandoned. He is not improvising.

The plan is intact—even in exile.

A Future and a Hope

What does "expected end" mean?

In Hebrew: אַחֲרִית וְתִקְוָה (acharit v'tikvah) — "a future and a hope."

This is not the guarantee of comfort—but the assurance of purpose.

Not immediate change—but ultimate restoration.

The people would return.

The temple would be rebuilt.

The covenant would be renewed.

And out of the ashes of Babylon would rise the line that led to Messiah.

This is the greater miracle:

> God doesn't just preserve His people in exile—He prepares redemption through it.

From Babylon, the path would one day lead to Bethlehem.

When You Seek Me

The promise continues:

> *"Then shall ye call upon Me... and ye shall seek Me, and find Me, when ye shall search for Me with all your heart."*
> *—Jeremiah 29:12-13*

Exile is not the end—it is the classroom of restored pursuit.

God was not interested in half-hearted devotion. He wanted all of them. A broken, desperate, purified hunger that cried: "We want You, not just Your blessings."

And the promise stands:

- Seek Me, and you will find Me.
- Call upon Me, and I will answer you.
- Search for Me—and I will reveal Myself again.

Even in Babylon.

Even after rebellion.

Even after judgment.

The door of return is never shut for the seeking heart.

A Letter for Us

This letter was addressed to ancient exiles—but its principles are eternal.

We, too, live in a kind of Babylon.

A world not our home.

A culture often hostile to truth.

A land of idols and confusion.

But even here, God's Word speaks:

- Build.
- Plant.
- Pray.
- Hope.
- Seek.
- Trust.

Because exile is not abandonment. It is a season of shaping, preparing, refining.

And the same God who sent the letter will one day bring us home.

Until then, we live like citizens of another Kingdom.

We labor in a foreign land, but with an eternal promise written on our hearts.

Let the letter speak again.

Let the ink of mercy remind you:

> God has not changed His mind about you.
>
> He knows His thoughts.
>
> And they are good.

thine word written on heart

CHAPTER XI
The Book of Consolation — A New Covenant Foretold

> *"I will write it in their hearts…"*
> — Jeremiah 31:33

After chapters of judgment, lament, and divine grief, there comes a radiant break in the clouds—a section of Jeremiah's prophecy so full of hope, so rich with promise, that scholars call it The Book of Consolation.

It spans chapters 30 to 33, and within it, the tone shifts. The fire of judgment does not disappear—but from its glow rises something more beautiful: a vision of restoration, redemption, and a covenant deeper than stone or scroll.

The message?

The God who disciplines is the same God who restores.

The Lord who uproots will also replant.

And the covenant that was broken will be rewritten—not with ink, but with fire upon the heart.

This is not just comfort for ancient Israel. It is the gospel in embryo, nestled within the ashes of exile.

"I Will Bring Again the Captivity"
The Book of Consolation opens with hope:

> *"I will bring again the captivity of My people Israel and Judah… and I will cause them to return to the land…"*
> — Jeremiah 30:3

God promises a return—not just to land, but to covenant relationship.

The exiles will come home.

The wounded will be healed.

The scattered will be gathered.

But this is not simply political restoration. It is spiritual revival.

God is not just undoing exile—He is unveiling a new future, shaped not by rebellion, but by righteousness.

The Days Are Coming
The refrain echoes through the chapters:

> *"Behold, the days come, saith the Lord..."*

This phrase signals not just a new season—but a new reality.

God is pointing toward a future that Israel could barely imagine.

- "I will be the God of all the families of Israel, and they shall be My people..." (Jeremiah 31:1)
- "Again I will build thee, and thou shalt be built, O virgin of Israel..." (Jeremiah 31:4)
- "I have loved thee with an everlasting love: therefore with lovingkindness have I drawn thee..." (Jeremiah 31:3)

This is not poetic filler. It is covenant fidelity.

> Even after betrayal, God speaks as a faithful Husband: "I still love you. And I will rebuild you."

Israel's sins did not nullify God's purposes.

Their failures did not cancel His faithfulness.

This is the comfort of the covenant-keeping God.

Rachel Weeping, and the Hope Beyond Tears
In the midst of this hope, we find a cry:

> *"A voice was heard in Ramah, lamentation, and bitter weeping; Rachel weeping for her children..."*
>
> *— Jeremiah 31:15*

It is a haunting image—Rachel, the matriarch of Israel, weeping over her lost descendants.

This verse would be echoed centuries later in Matthew 2, as Herod slaughtered the children of Bethlehem. Jeremiah's words became a prophecy of another sorrow—another exile—another deliverance.

But even in the lament, there is hope:

> *"Refrain thy voice from weeping... thy work shall be rewarded... they shall come again from the land of the enemy."*
>
> *— Jeremiah 31:16*

Tears are not the final word.

Exile is not the end of the story.

There is still reward. Still return. Still redemption.

This is consolation that stretches beyond generations.

The New Covenant

Then comes the heart of the promise. A covenant unlike anything before:

> *"Behold, the days come, saith the Lord, that I will make a new covenant with the house of Israel, and with the house of Judah..."*
>
> *— Jeremiah 31:31*

This is radical.

The old covenant—written on stone at Sinai, mediated by Moses, sealed with blood—had been broken again and again. The people failed to obey. Their hearts wandered. Their hands built idols. Their mouths spoke lies.

But now, God offers something new.

Not another law.

Not another ritual.

Not another scroll.

But a new nature.

> *"I will put My law in their inward parts, and write it in their hearts; and will be their God, and they shall be My people."*
>
> *— Jeremiah 31:33*

This is the gospel before the Gospels.

A new covenant, fulfilled in Jesus Christ, sealed by His blood, and written on the heart by the Holy Spirit.

Paul would later call us:

> "epistles written not with ink, but with the Spirit of the living God" —2 Corinthians 3:3.

Hebrews 8 and 10 would quote this very chapter to declare that Jesus is the Mediator of a better covenant—one that could not be broken by man because it was fulfilled by God Himself.

Forgiveness that Forgets

> "For I will forgive their iniquity, and I will remember their sin no more."
>
> — *Jeremiah 31:34*

This is not amnesia—it is divine choice.

God chooses to no longer hold the record.

The holy Judge becomes the merciful Father.

The One who could condemn now covers.

This is the climax of the consolation:

- Return from exile.
- Renewal of relationship.
- Rewriting of the law.
- Removal of sin's record.

Not because Israel earned it.

But because God loved them still.

Fields Bought in Anathoth

In Jeremiah 32, the prophet—still imprisoned—receives an unusual instruction: buy a field.

Even as Jerusalem is under siege, and Babylon is breaching the walls, God tells Jeremiah to purchase land in Anathoth, his hometown.

Why?

Because God is planting hope in the soil of despair.

> "Houses and fields and vineyards shall be possessed again in this land."
>
> — *Jeremiah 32:15*

It is a prophetic act.

A stake in the promise.

A declaration that this devastation is temporary.

Jeremiah signs the deed.

Places it in an earthen jar.

And stores it as a witness to future restoration.

The message is clear:

Even in prison.

Even in ruins.

Even when all seems lost— God is still writing the future.

A City Called the Lord Our Righteousness

The Book of Consolation closes with a vision of a restored Davidic throne:

> *"I will raise unto David a righteous Branch, and a King shall reign and prosper..."*
>
> *— Jeremiah 23:5; echoed in 33:15*

And the name of this King?

"The Lord our Righteousness" — יְהוָה צִדְקֵנוּ (YHWH Tzidkenu)

This is a prophecy of Messiah.

Not just another king. Not just another priest.

But One who would embody the righteousness of God.

Who would rule in justice.

And who would become our righteousness (see 1 Corinthians 1:30).

This is Christ.

Born into exile.

Risen as the fulfillment.

The living New Covenant.

The Righteous Branch.

The Word written not on stone—but in flesh.

The Scroll of Comfort Still Speaks

The Book of Consolation is not just ancient poetry.

It is a declaration for every exiled heart.

A promise to every captive soul.

A whisper of mercy in the middle of mourning.

It tells us:

- God has not abandoned you.
- The covenant is not over.
- The future is not lost.
- And your sin can be forgiven. Fully. Freely. Forever.

Let the scroll speak again.

Let the new covenant be written not just in doctrine—but in your very spirit.

Let the hope of Jeremiah be the joy of your salvation.

Because consolation has a name—And His name is Jesus.

CHAPTER XII
Jeremiah and the Remnant — The Ones Who Fled

Egypt-bound fugitives who refused to obey
The city had fallen. The walls were breached. The temple lay in ashes. Babylon had conquered what was once the pride of Zion.

For most of Judah, exile had become reality.

But a small group remained—a remnant, fragile and uncertain, clinging to the soil of a devastated homeland. This remnant had survived the sword, the siege, and the fire. One might assume they would now cling to God with trembling devotion.

But what happens next is one of the most heartbreaking turns in Jeremiah's ministry.

They refused to listen. Again.

This chapter explores not the stubbornness of kings or the rebellion of crowds, but the tragic disobedience of those who should have known better—the very few who remained after judgment had run its course.

They had every reason to obey.

But they ran.

To Egypt.

And Jeremiah, old and grieving, followed them to deliver one final word.

The Remnant That Survived
After the fall of Jerusalem in 586 BC, Babylon left behind a small number of survivors—farmers, artisans, and civilians—under the governorship of Gedaliah. He was appointed to oversee the land and preserve order.

For a brief moment, there was a flicker of hope.

A chance to rebuild.

A sliver of mercy after the storm.

But chaos quickly returned.

Gedaliah was assassinated by Ishmael, a Judean nobleman. Fear spread like wildfire. The people panicked. They feared Babylon would return to punish them for the murder.

So they approached Jeremiah—the prophet they had ignored for years—and begged for guidance.

> *"Pray for us unto the Lord thy God... that the Lord thy God may show us the way wherein we may walk..."*
>
> *— Jeremiah 42:2-3*

At last, it seemed, they were ready to listen.

They even made a vow:

> *"Whether it be good, or whether it be evil, we will obey the voice of the Lord..."*
>
> *— Jeremiah 42:6*

But it was a lie.

Ten Days of Silence

Jeremiah prayed.

He waited.

Ten days passed before the Word of the Lord came.

When it did, it was clear:

- Stay in the land, and God will bless and protect you.
- Do not go down to Egypt, for there, sword, famine, and death await.
- Trust Me, even though things look fragile.
- Fear not, for Babylon will not consume you if you remain.

It was not what they expected.

They wanted escape.

God offered endurance.

They wanted security.

God offered surrender.

And then the veil dropped.

They never intended to obey.

The Lie Exposed
Upon hearing the word, the people responded with venom:

> *"Thou speakest falsely: the Lord our God hath not sent thee..."*
>
> — *Jeremiah 43:2*

The very prophet they had begged for help was now accused of lying.

They rejected the message, denied the Lord's voice, and chose Egypt over obedience.

Jeremiah was taken by force, dragged with them into Egypt. Even in disobedience, they couldn't leave him behind. God ensured His prophet would still speak, even in exile.

This remnant, meant to be the seed of restoration, became a symbol of rebellion all over again.

The cycle continued.

They broke their promise.

They fled the covenant.

They escaped the judgment—only to run back into it.

Egypt: The Old Slavery Revisited
Egypt was more than a geographic location—it was a symbol of regression.

Israel had once been delivered from Egypt by mighty miracles.

Now, in fear and unbelief, the remnant returned.

The place of slavery became their refuge.

The land of former bondage became their escape route.

This is the tragedy of unbelief:

When faith is hard, familiar chains feel safer than foreign trust.

But God sees. And God speaks.

In Egypt, Jeremiah delivers one of his final words:

> *"Behold, I will send and take Nebuchadnezzar the king of Babylon, My servant… and he shall smite the land of Egypt…"*
>
> *— Jeremiah 43:10*

Even Egypt would not save them.

Judgment would follow them there.

There is no safety outside of obedience.

The Worship of the Queen of Heaven

In Jeremiah 44, the Lord confronts the final apostasy of the remnant: idolatry.

Despite all they had witnessed—siege, famine, fire, exile—they still burned incense to false gods. Specifically, the Queen of Heaven, a pagan fertility goddess.

God, through Jeremiah, confronts them with history:

> *"Have ye forgotten the wickedness of your fathers…? They are not humbled even unto this day…"*
>
> *— Jeremiah 44:9-10*

Their reply is jaw-dropping:

> *"As for the word that thou hast spoken unto us in the name of the Lord, we will not hearken unto thee."*
>
> *— Jeremiah 44:16*

> *They even claimed that when they worshiped the Queen of Heaven, "we had plenty of victuals, and were well, and saw no evil."*
>
> *— Jeremiah 44:17*

They attributed blessing to idolatry.

They refused accountability.

They chose comfort over covenant.

And sealed their fate.

The Remnant Rejected
God's final word to them was devastating:

> *"Behold, I have sworn by My great name... that My name shall no more be named in the mouth of any man of Judah in all the land of Egypt..."*
>
> *— Jeremiah 44:26*

It was a form of divine disowning.

God removed His name from their lips.

The covenant, for them, was sealed in rebellion.

They would die in Egypt—unheard, unremembered, unredeemed.

The remnant that should have been the beginning of restoration chose their own way—and perished.

Lessons from a Fleeing Remnant
This chapter of Jeremiah's life is one of his most sorrowful.

He had endured the mockery of kings, the dungeons of princes, the rejection of priests—only to be dragged into exile by those who claimed they would obey.

Yet he remained faithful.

He spoke.

He wept.

He warned.

He watched them fall.

And from his obedience comes this sobering truth:

- Hearing the Word is not the same as obeying it.
- Asking for guidance means nothing if the heart is set on its own way.
- God sees through pious words and exposes our true intent.
- Fleeing from judgment never works when the root is disobedience.

We, too, are a kind of remnant.

And we must ask:

- Will we stay in the land of promise, even when it's hard?
- Will we obey when God says "wait" instead of "escape"?
- Will we trust the slow path of restoration over the easy road of rebellion?

Let us not be the ones who flee to Egypt in the name of safety.

Let us be the ones who stay planted, who seek peace, who obey with trembling reverence.

Because the safest place to be—is wherever God said to remain.

CHAPTER XIII
Foreshadows of the Christ — The Righteous Branch

> *"Behold, the days come, saith the Lord, that I will raise unto David a righteous Branch..."*
>
> — *Jeremiah 23:5*

Though Jeremiah's prophecies are heavy with judgment, lament, and national collapse, they are also bright with flashes of divine promise—especially regarding the future King who would rise from the ashes of David's ruined dynasty.

That King is not just a monarch.

He is a Messiah.

Jeremiah, often seen as the prophet of tears, is also a herald of hope—a seer who looks beyond Babylon, beyond the shattered temple, beyond the broken covenant, and sees a Branch, springing from a cut-down tree.

This Branch is not weak.

Not fragile.

Not temporal.

He is righteous.

He is eternal.

He is the fulfillment of every covenant God ever made.

And His name?

"The Lord Our Righteousness"

YHWH Tzidkenu — יְהוָה צִדְקֵנוּ

This is not just a title.

It is a revelation of Jesus Christ, centuries before the cradle of Bethlehem.

A Righteous Branch from a Cut-Down Line

> *"Behold, the days come... I will raise unto David a righteous Branch..."*
>
> *— Jeremiah 23:5*

By the time of Jeremiah, the Davidic dynasty had decayed.

Kings were corrupt.

Judgment had come.

Zedekiah—the last king of Judah—was about to fall.

The house of David looked like a dead stump.

But God never forgets His promises.

Isaiah had prophesied earlier:

> *"And there shall come forth a rod out of the stem of Jesse, and a Branch shall grow out of his roots."*
>
> *— Isaiah 11:1*

Same image.

A shoot. A tender sprout from a felled tree.

Life where there was only ruin.

Jeremiah continues:

> *"And a King shall reign and prosper, and shall execute judgment and justice in the earth."*
>
> *— Jeremiah 23:5*

This is no ordinary king.

He rules in righteousness.

He governs in peace.

He restores what sin destroyed.

The Name: YHWH Tzidkenu

> *"And this is His name whereby He shall be called, THE LORD OUR RIGHTEOUSNESS."*
>
> — *Jeremiah 23:6*

This is stunning.

In the Hebrew: יְהוָה צִדְקֵנוּ (YHWH Tzidkenu)

God's personal name—YHWH—is joined with the concept of righteousness (tzedek).

This King is righteousness.

Not just a representative of it.

Not just a preacher of it.

Not just a symbol of it.

He embodies it.

And more than that: He becomes ours.

> *"The Lord OUR Righteousness."*

We do not just admire Him—we are covered by Him.

This is the heart of the gospel, prophesied by Jeremiah:

That one day, a righteous King would give His righteousness to His people.

Paul would later write:

> *"For He hath made Him to be sin for us... that we might be made the righteousness of God in Him."*
>
> — *2 Corinthians 5:21*

Jesus is not just righteous—He is our righteousness.

In His Days Judah Shall Be Saved

The promise continues:

> *"In His days Judah shall be saved, and Israel shall dwell safely..."*
>
> — *Jeremiah 23:6*

This is national restoration.

A reunited kingdom.

A healed covenant.

But more than that—it is spiritual salvation.

The salvation Jeremiah points to goes deeper than geography or borders.

It is salvation from sin.

From rebellion.

From the deep-rooted unrighteousness that led to exile in the first place.

Jesus fulfills this not only by restoring Israel spiritually, but by grafting in Gentiles, forming one new man (—Ephesians 2:15).

The Righteous Branch is the root of Jesse, the son of David, and the Savior of all nations.

The New Exodus
Jeremiah expands the vision in chapter 23:

> *"Therefore, behold, the days come... that they shall no more say, The Lord liveth, which brought up the children of Israel out of the land of Egypt; But, The Lord liveth, which brought up and led the seed of the house of Israel out of the north country..."*
>
> *—Jeremiah 23:7–8*

The Exodus from Egypt was the defining act of salvation in Israel's history.

But Jeremiah says another exodus is coming—greater, deeper, final.

It is the exodus from sin.

From judgment.

From the exile of the heart.

And it would be accomplished by the Branch.

This King would not come with chariots.

He would come riding on a donkey.

He would not destroy Rome—He would destroy death.

He would not ascend to a golden throne—but to a bloody cross.

And there, righteousness would be transferred.

Not earned.

Given.

YHWH Tzidkenu—The Lord Our Righteousness—would take our sin and robe us in His glory.

The Promise Reaffirmed
Jeremiah returns to this theme in chapter 33:

> *"I will cause the Branch of righteousness to grow up unto David... In those days shall Judah be saved... and this is the name wherewith she shall be called, The Lord our righteousness."*
>
> — *Jeremiah 33:15–16*

This time, Jerusalem herself shares the name.

Not just the Messiah, but His people.

His righteousness is imputed, shared, bestowed.

> We don't just worship the Lord our Righteousness—we become the righteousness of God in Him.

This is the miracle of grace.

From Prophecy to Person
Jeremiah never lived to see the Branch.

He died in exile, likely in Egypt, still speaking truth to a people who rejected him.

But his words lived on.

And 600 years later, a baby was born in Bethlehem.

A Branch.

A King.

A Righteous Redeemer.

He would be baptized in the Jordan.

Preach in the towns of Galilee.

Weep over Jerusalem.

Be betrayed, bruised, crucified.

And then rise again.

The Branch had come.

And He still reigns.

Do You Know the Righteous Branch?

Jeremiah's vision of the Messiah is not poetic myth.

It is prophetic fire.

It burns through time and asks each generation:

- Do you still trust in your own righteousness?
- Are you trying to build your own crown?
- Or have you bowed to the Branch?
- Have you received His righteousness as your own?

Because the name is still His:

YHWH Tzidkenu

The Lord our Righteousness.

And that name is offered to all who believe.

Not because you are worthy—But because He is.

CHAPTER XIV
The Prophet and the Pit — A Life of Rejection

Thrown into cisterns but never abandoned by God
Jeremiah was not just a prophet of words—he was a prophet of wounds.

Few in Scripture lived the burden of divine calling with such raw exposure, such visible suffering. His entire life became a living sermon. While others prophesied from platforms of power or praised the king to gain favor, Jeremiah's pulpit was a pit. His sanctuary was a prison. His reward was rejection.

He wasn't honored with robes.

He was clothed in chains.

He wasn't celebrated.

He was accused, beaten, mocked, and thrown into a cistern.

But God had chosen him from the womb for this—A ministry of truth in isolation, Of hope in humiliation, Of light in the shadows of a collapsing world.

This is the prophet who kept standing, even while sinking into the mud.

The Price of Truth
By the time Jerusalem was under siege, Jeremiah had already delivered decades of warning. His words were like fire—but most hearts were stone. He had shattered the illusions of the people's false peace. He had rebuked kings, priests, and prophets. And now, as Babylon circled the city like a vulture, Jeremiah's warnings became unbearable to the ruling elite.

Zedekiah, the king, was weak-willed—pulled between his fear of Babylon and his fear of the people. He allowed Jeremiah to live but refused to heed his message.

When Jeremiah declared that the only path to life was surrender to Babylon, it was seen as treason.

"He weakeneth the hands of the men of war…" (Jeremiah 38:4)

They accused him of sedition, of breaking the spirit of the people during wartime.

Truth had become a threat. The Word of the Lord was now an enemy.

Lowered into the Pit
So they silenced him.

> *"Then took they Jeremiah, and cast him into the dungeon of Malchiah… and they let down Jeremiah with cords. And in the dungeon there was no water, but mire: so Jeremiah sunk in the mire."*
>
> — *Jeremiah 38:6*

This was no symbolic metaphor.

It was a literal cistern—a deep, muddy pit. No floor, no light, no exit.

A place of slow death.

This was where truth ended up.

Not in the palace. Not on the scroll.

But in the pit.

The prophet who had wept for the nation was now left to die in silence.

He sank—slowly—into the mud.

Yet even here, Jeremiah teaches us something:

Faith is not proven on the platform, but in the pit.

When all comforts are stripped, when the world turns its back, when the mission looks like failure—faith must decide: Do I still trust God, or not?

Jeremiah trusted.

Even in the mud.

A Voice Still Heard
But God had not forgotten.

While the leaders of Jerusalem schemed, God stirred the heart of an unlikely advocate: Ebed-melech, an Ethiopian eunuch in the king's house.

He heard what had been done and went directly to the king:

> *"My lord the king, these men have done evil in all that they have done to Jeremiah the prophet…"*
>
> *— Jeremiah 38:9*

Zedekiah, ever passive, gave permission.

Ebed-melech gathered old rags and ropes and went to rescue the prophet.

> *"Put these old cast clouts and rotten rags under thine armholes under the cords."*
>
> *— Jeremiah 38:12*

Even in rescue, there is tenderness.

Ebed-melech didn't yank him out carelessly.

He cushioned the cords so Jeremiah's frail body wouldn't be torn.

Even when the world rejects you, God still knows how to send help.

Even when your enemies outnumber you, God can send one eunuch, one rope, one word—and your deliverance comes.

Jeremiah was lifted from the pit—not promoted, not applauded, but preserved.

A Prophet Rejected by All
Jeremiah's life never turned glamorous.

He never saw the fruit of his preaching in his lifetime.

He never had a revival.

He never had peace.

He remained an outcast, a weeper, a wanderer.

But heaven recorded his faithfulness.

The same man who sank in the mire would later be quoted by Jesus Christ Himself.

Jeremiah, whose words fell on deaf ears in Jerusalem, became a foundational voice in the gospel story.

Jeremiah prophesied rejection—Jesus fulfilled it.

Jeremiah wept over Jerusalem—Jesus wept for her too.

Jeremiah was betrayed by his own—so was the Messiah.

Jeremiah was cast into a pit—Jesus into a tomb.

Both emerged—one lifted by cords, the other by resurrection.

Called to Be Faithful, Not Famous
Jeremiah was never called to popularity.

He was called to perseverance.

He was never promised success.

He was promised suffering.

But he endured.

And in doing so, he shows every believer:

- Obedience may land you in the pit.
- Faithfulness may mean walking alone.
- Truth may get you thrown out.
- But you are never forgotten by God.

In Jeremiah's rejection, we see a preview of the rejected Stone who would become the Cornerstone.

And if you are walking through your own pit—if your calling has led to loneliness, or your obedience has invited rejection—then you are not off course.

You are on the same path the prophets walked.

And Christ walks with you still.

A Word from the Mud

If the prophet could speak from the mire, maybe this is what he'd say:

Don't measure your calling by applause.

Don't trade your conviction for comfort.

Even in the darkest pit, God sees, God speaks, and God will raise you up.

Let the pit refine you.

Let rejection sanctify you.

Let the voice of God be louder than the crowd's silence.

Because some of the purest words ever spoken came from a man sinking in the mud, holding on to a God who never let go.

כוס חמת יהוה

Translation: The Cup of the Wrath of the LORD

CHAPTER XV
Jeremiah's Final Word — The Cup of God's Wrath

Nations judged, kingdoms shaken, truth unburied

At the end of Jeremiah's prophetic journey, the weeping ceases. The pleadings quiet. The window for repentance closes. Now comes the final word—not just for Judah, but for the nations.

This is not Jeremiah's opinion.

This is the cup of God's wrath, passed from one kingdom to another.

The prophet, often known for lament and compassion, now speaks as the Lord's appointed messenger of judgment.

And judgment does not discriminate.

From Jerusalem to Egypt, from Edom to Babylon, the cup is passed—and none are exempt.

The Command to Carry the Cup

In Jeremiah 25, the prophet receives a solemn instruction:

> *"Take the wine cup of this fury at My hand, and cause all the nations, to whom I send thee, to drink it."*
>
> —*Jeremiah 25:15*

This is no symbolic gesture.

This is a heavenly decree of consequence.

The cup represents divine wrath—measured, righteous, and inescapable. It is poured out not in rage, but in justice.

The Lord declares that these nations must drink—even if they refuse:

> *"They shall drink, and be moved, and be mad, because of the sword that I will send among them." (v.16)*

This is the same God who once passed a cup of blessing to His people in covenant.

Now, it is the cup of fury—because the covenant has been trampled.

This cup flows through history.

It is the overflow of human rebellion, injustice, idolatry, and bloodshed.

And Jeremiah is called to carry it—not as a priest, but as a prophet.

The Cup Touches Every Nation

The list of nations in Jeremiah 25 is extensive and intentional. It includes:

- Jerusalem and Judah – God's own people are first in line. Judgment begins at the house of God.
- Egypt – The symbol of past bondage and future false alliances.
- Philistines – Longtime enemies, coastal powers.
- Edom, Moab, Ammon – Descendants of Abraham's family, corrupted by pride and perversion.
- Tyre and Sidon – Merchants of greed and self-exaltation.
- Dedan, Tema, Buz – Distant desert tribes, none beyond God's reach.
- Elam and Media – Eastern empires soon to rise in power.
- Babylon – The final cupbearer, great and terrible, yet not immune.

This sweeping judgment teaches one eternal truth:

No throne is safe from the justice of God.

The cup touches the powerful and the petty, the religious and the pagan, the near and the far.

No borders, treaties, alliances, or idols can shield from the One who judges with perfect righteousness.

Roar from the Holy Habitation

Jeremiah's vision intensifies:

> *"The Lord shall roar from on high... He shall mightily roar upon His habitation... A noise shall come even to the ends of the earth..."*
>
> —*Jeremiah 25:30–31*

This is cosmic judgment.

The Lion of Judah is no longer silent.

He roars—not just at sin, but for the vindication of His holiness.

And when God roars, even the earth trembles.

- This is not the whisper of a grieving father.
- This is not the warning of a reluctant prophet.
- This is the war cry of heaven.

"He will plead with all flesh; He will give them that are wicked to the sword."

This is not a random outburst. It is divine litigation.

The Creator is holding His creation to account.

The Slain of the Lord

Jeremiah records a chilling reality:

> *"And the slain of the Lord shall be at that day from one end of the earth even unto the other..." (v.33)*

This is not poetic exaggeration.

This is prophetic reckoning.

It speaks to the Day of the Lord, the time when human systems collapse under the weight of divine truth.

In Revelation, this same cup appears:

> *"The great city... made all nations drink of the wine of the wrath of her fornication."*
>
> —*Revelation 14:8*

Jeremiah and John see the same vision—centuries apart.

The cup passed through history eventually finds its fulfillment in the judgment of all nations.

But There Is Another Cup
Yet this chapter of wrath cannot be read rightly unless we also see another cup.

Hundreds of years after Jeremiah, another man—greater than the prophet—enters a garden. He too is trembling. He too is facing judgment.

"Father, if it be possible, let this cup pass from Me..."

—Matthew 26:39

This cup was not passed to the nations—It was passed to one man:

Jesus.

The Righteous Branch.

The Lamb.

And He drank it.

The fury meant for all of us—He took it.

The judgment prophesied in Jeremiah—He bore it.

The wrath due to the nations—He absorbed it.

He did not pass it.

He drained it.

For us.

This is the mystery of redemption:

The prophet brings the cup—but the Messiah drinks it.

Final Words, Eternal Echoes
Jeremiah's final word is not popular.

It is not soft.

It is not marketable.

But it is true.

- God will judge every idol.
- He will confront every injustice.
- He will silence every false voice.
- And He will bring down every throne not built on righteousness.

The cup will not go away.

But because of Christ, we are offered a new cup—the cup of the new covenant in His blood (—Luke 22:20).

You will drink from one of them.

The cup of wrath—or the cup of mercy.

The cup of judgment—or the cup of grace.

And the choice is offered freely.

Jeremiah's Legacy
He was not famous in his day.

But heaven remembers him.

He was not loved by his people.

But he was held by God.

He wept over sin.

He spoke the truth.

He suffered for the Word.

And he never stopped pointing toward the One who would come and make it all right.

Jeremiah's final word is not only about wrath—It's about truth unburied, Hope untouched, And a righteous King who will have the final word.

APPENDIX

Timeline of Jeremiah's Ministry

640 BCE — 609 BCE — 597 BCE

Josiah | Jehoiakim | Zedekiah

Josiah — Jeremiah — Jeremiah Called as Prophet — Fall of Jerusalem — Rema

First Siege of Jerusalem

DC

SCRIPTURE INDEX

Jeremiah 1:5
Chapter 1: The Call Before Collapse — A Prophet Is Formed

Jeremiah 2:27
Chapter 9: The Broken Covenant — Judah's Spiritual Adultery

Jeremiah 7:4
Chapter 4: The Temple Sermon — When Religion Becomes Rebellion

Jeremiah 9
Chapter 7: Weeping Over a City That Would Not Listen

Jeremiah 18:2
Chapter 8: The Potter's House — Vessels of Glory or Destruction

Jeremiah 18:6
Chapter 8: The Potter's House — Vessels of Glory or Destruction

Jeremiah 19:11
Chapter 8: The Potter's House — Vessels of Glory or Destruction

Jeremiah 20:9
Chapter 2: Burning Words in a Shaking World — Jeremiah's Fire Within

Jeremiah 23:5
Chapter 13: Foreshadows of the Christ — The Righteous Branch

Jeremiah 25:15
Chapter 15: Jeremiah's Final Word — The Cup of God's Wrath

Jeremiah 25:16
Chapter 15: Jeremiah's Final Word — The Cup of God's Wrath

Jeremiah 25:30–31
Chapter 15: Jeremiah's Final Word — The Cup of God's Wrath

Jeremiah 25:33
Chapter 15: Jeremiah's Final Word — The Cup of God's Wrath

Jeremiah 27
Chapter 5: The Yoke of Babylon — Submission as Sovereignty

Jeremiah 28
Chapter 3: False Prophets and Broken Altars — Exposing the Lie

Jeremiah 29:11
Chapter 10: Letters from Exile — Hope in Captivity

Jeremiah 31:33
Chapter 11: The Book of Consolation — A New Covenant Foretold

Jeremiah 36
Chapter 6: The Scroll Was Burned — But the Word Returned

Jeremiah 38:4
Chapter 14: The Prophet and the Pit — A Life of Rejection

Jeremiah 38:6
Chapter 14: The Prophet and the Pit — A Life of Rejection

Jeremiah 38:9
Chapter 14: The Prophet and the Pit — A Life of Rejection

Jeremiah 38:12
Chapter 14: The Prophet and the Pit — A Life of Rejection

Jeremiah 42–44
Chapter 12: Jeremiah and the Remnant — The Ones Who Fled

Lamentations 1
Chapter 7: Weeping Over a City That Would Not Listen

Matthew 26:39
Chapter 14: The Prophet and the Pit — A Life of Rejection;
Chapter 15: Jeremiah's Final Word — The Cup of God's Wrath

Luke 22:20
Chapter 15: Jeremiah's Final Word — The Cup of God's Wrath

Romans 9
Chapter 8: The Potter's House — Vessels of Glory or Destruction

Revelation 14:8
Chapter 15: Jeremiah's Final Word — The Cup of God's Wrath

GLOSSARY OF TERMS

Adultery, Spiritual
A biblical metaphor describing unfaithfulness to God, often used by prophets like Jeremiah to rebuke Israel and Judah for idolatry, disobedience, and breaking covenant with the Lord.

Baruch
The faithful scribe of Jeremiah who recorded his prophetic words and stood by him through persecution and rejection. Instrumental in preserving Jeremiah's scroll when it was burned by King Jehoiakim.

Babylon
The rising empire during Jeremiah's time, used by God as an instrument of judgment against Judah. Symbolizes both a historical oppressor and a prophetic picture of worldly rebellion against God.

Burning Fire (Jeremiah 20:9)
Jeremiah's description of the unstoppable force of God's word within him—a divine compulsion to speak truth even when it brought pain.

Covenant
A binding spiritual agreement between God and His people. Jeremiah often speaks of the broken covenant and prophesies a new covenant written on the heart (Jeremiah 31:33).

Cup of Wrath
A symbol of divine judgment. God instructs Jeremiah to make the nations drink from this cup as a sign of their coming judgment (Jeremiah 25). It finds its ultimate fulfillment in Christ, who drank the cup on our behalf (Matthew 26:39).

False Prophets
Deceivers who contradicted God's true message by speaking peace when there was none. Jeremiah battled voices like Hananiah, who falsely promised deliverance from Babylon.

Hananiah
A false prophet in Jeremiah 28 who claimed God would break Babylon's yoke in two years. He was publicly refuted by Jeremiah and died shortly after as God had declared.

Jeremiah
The weeping prophet called before birth, chosen to speak God's truth to a rebellious nation during one of its darkest times. He prophesied the fall of Jerusalem, urged repentance, and foretold the new covenant.

Jehoiakim
King of Judah who defied Jeremiah and burned the original scroll of his prophecies. His actions symbolized the nation's rejection of God's word.

Judgment
A central theme of the book—God's righteous intervention against sin, idolatry, and injustice. Jeremiah emphasizes that judgment begins with God's people but extends to all nations.

Lamentations
A poetic book traditionally attributed to Jeremiah, written after the destruction of Jerusalem. It gives voice to sorrow, loss, and the faithful mourning of a prophet who loved his people.

New Covenant
Prophesied by Jeremiah as a future promise in which God's law would be written not on tablets but on human hearts (Jeremiah 31:31–33). Fulfilled through Christ.

Potter's House
Jeremiah's vision of a potter shaping clay symbolizes God's sovereign authority to form, reshape, or judge nations. The image warns that hardened clay will be broken (Jeremiah 18–19).

Prophet
One who speaks on behalf of God. In Jeremiah's case, this included calling nations to repentance, pronouncing judgment, and offering hope.

Remnant
The faithful few who survive judgment and remain loyal to God. Jeremiah's message to the remnant was both correction and comfort.

Righteous Branch
A messianic title used by Jeremiah (Jeremiah 23:5) to foretell the coming of a king from David's line who would reign in justice and righteousness—fulfilled in Christ Jesus.

Scroll
A written record of Jeremiah's prophecies, initially destroyed by the king but rewritten by God's instruction (Jeremiah 36). Symbol of the indestructibility of God's word.

Temple Sermon
A bold prophetic message delivered by Jeremiah in the temple gates (Jeremiah 7), exposing the people's false reliance on the temple as a guarantee of security.

The Word of the Lord
The divine voice that came repeatedly to Jeremiah, shaping every chapter of his ministry. It was not just heard but burned like fire in his bones.

The Yoke of Babylon
A prophetic symbol (Jeremiah 27) illustrating Judah's coming subjugation under Babylon's rule. Jeremiah urged submission—not out of defeat, but as obedience to God's will.

ACKNOWLEDGEMENTS

First and foremost, I offer eternal thanks to the Lord God Almighty—the One who called Jeremiah before he was formed in the womb, and who calls each of us to stand, to speak, and to weep for a generation in need of truth. May every word in this book be a reflection of Your voice, and may it carry the weight of Your fire.

To Yeshua, the Righteous Branch, who not only fulfilled the prophecies of Jeremiah but bore the cup of wrath so that mercy could flow. You are the Word in my bones, the tears behind every lament, and the joy that waits on the other side of obedience.

To the Holy Spirit, the One who stirred the prophet's heart and now breathes through the pages of Scripture—thank You for awakening my understanding and kindling the fire of intercession and boldness within me.

To Feebe, my beloved wife—your unwavering encouragement, discernment, and spiritual insight have been a lamp in dark places. Thank you for walking beside me through seasons of rejection, revelation, and resolve. This book carries your prayers in every chapter.

To my father, who has always seen the unseen and heard God in the silence—your legacy is in every page I write. And to my mother, who taught me how to weep for a broken world and to believe in a God who restores.

To Greg Laurie and all those shepherds who proclaim Christ without compromise—thank you for reminding us that the voice of a prophet still echoes through faithful preaching, and that revival comes through repentance.

To the remnant believers across the nations—those who still tremble at God's Word, who endure rejection for truth, who carry scrolls no one wants to read: this book is for you.

To my global family—those in Israel, Pakistan, Italy, Jordan, the United States, and beyond—your hunger for the Word and your cries for the Spirit's move continue to inspire this work.

To my publishing and design partners, and every reader who has carried these pages into their hearts—may you find in Jeremiah's journey a mirror for your own calling, your own fire, and your own tears.

Finally, to every soul who has ever stood in the cracks of a collapsing culture—misunderstood, isolated, and yet faithful—may you know this:

You are not forgotten. You are not alone. You were called before the foundations.

Just like Jeremiah.

— Damiano B. Centola

ABOUT THE AUTHOR

Damiano B. Centola is a visionary author, poetic theologian, and prophetic voice whose works ignite a hunger for truth and a return to the holy fire of God. His writings carry the weight of Scripture, the beauty of language, and the urgency of the times—calling a generation to repentance, renewal, and courageous obedience.

With a heart for the remnant and a deep reverence for the Word of God, Damiano has authored over thirty books that traverse sacred themes such as divine sovereignty, spiritual corruption, the names of God, biblical design, the bloodline of redemption, and the prophetic seasons of Israel. His voice speaks both to the ancient paths and the modern battlefield—bridging Scripture, art, theology, and truth with striking clarity and power.

In Jeremiah: The Prophet Between the Cracks of a Broken Nation, Damiano offers a raw and Spirit-breathed journey through the life of the weeping prophet—a journey not only into history, but into the soul of every believer who stands for truth when the world turns away.

Damiano writes not to be seen, but to help others see—see the Word more clearly, the times more soberly, and the Lord more intimately. His pen bears the weight of intercession, and his works are marked not by ambition, but by divine assignment.

He lives with his wife Feebe Huang—his greatest earthly companion and intercessor—and together they walk out the call to speak, write, build, and burn for God's glory across nations.

For more books, teachings, and prophetic resources, visit:
www.damianocentola.com

www.ingramcontent.com/pod-product-compliance
Lightning Source LLC
Chambersburg PA
CBHW061221070526
44584CB00029B/3925